Hitler

Also by Norman Stone

The Eastern Front 1914–1917

Hitler

Norman Stone

with an Introduction by
J. H. Plumb

LITTLE, BROWN AND COMPANY   BOSTON   TORONTO

FIRST EDITION

All photographs courtesy of The Imperial War Museum, London

LIBRARY OF CONGRESS CATALOGING IN PUBLICATION DATA

Stone, Norman.
  Hitler.

  Includes bibliographical references and index.
    1. Hitler, Adolf, 1889–1945. 2. Heads of
state—Germany—Biography. 3. Germany—History—
1933–1945. 4. National socialism—History.
DD247.H5S778   943.086′092′4 [B]   80–357
ISBN 0–316–81757–0

MV

Designed by D. Christine Benders

*Published simultaneously in Canada
by Little, Brown & Company (Canada) Limited*

PRINTED IN THE UNITED STATES OF AMERICA

For my mother, Mary Stone,
in remembrance of what Hitler's war has caused us both

Contents

Introduction

TO MEN AND WOMEN of my generation Hitler was the curse of our youth and early adulthood, the black blight that lay across our future — and a blight that crept steadily nearer. The prospects of self-imposed exile or death were not rhetorical ideas of fervid imagination but possible contingencies, events that had to be thought about, events that drew closer and closer as the reoccupation of the Rhineland was followed not only by that of Austria and Czechoslovakia but also by the long, agonizing defeat of the Spanish Republic. Hope was almost impossible to sustain; and, with growing knowledge of Hitler's treatment of Jews, gypsies, and liberals, Hitler turned into the embodiment of evil. Bred in the knowledge of the Somme and Passchendaele, we saw war as nothing but terrible and loathsome, yet, when war at last came in 1939, all were filled with joy. Hope came flooding back so strongly that not even the defeats of 1940 and 1941 could wipe it out. The trauma of Hitler stretched over fifteen years for my generation, breaking lives, destroying those one loved, wrecking my country. So it has been difficult, well-nigh impossible, to think calmly of that white, mustachioed face, eyes ablaze like a Charlie Chaplin turned into a nightmare. Even now when I recall that face and hear that terrifying, hysterical, screeching voice, they create a sense of approaching doom, disaster, and death.

Yet, hard though it may be, Hitler has to be understood, and to do so, one needs a historian of both Norman Stone's quality and generation for, by the time Norman Stone became a professional historian, Hitler was a part of history and the Germany of Brandt and Schmidt had sprung from the ruins of Hitler's Reich. Hence there is a detachment, an irony, and an understanding in his life of Hitler which, I think, no one of my generation has or could achieve.

And the great merit of Stone's book is that it makes one realize the positive qualities of Hitler, his real achievements and the basis for his immense popularity, without ever losing sight of the tenth-rate quality of his political thinking, the personal squalor and inadequacy of most of his supporters, or the inhumanity of so many of his actions and policies.

It may come as a surprise to many to learn of the weakness of Germany's armies right up to 1940 and even beyond, or that most of Hitler's actions were opportunistic rather than carefully calculated (yet, of course, always set in a cloudy vision of Aryan world domination) and that his outstanding victories were due more to Allied incompetence and lack of will than to Hitler's planning and skill. Yet Stone never underestimates the extraordinary capacity of Hitler to dominate Germany's army, so completely, indeed, that there was no widespread collapse even to the end.

Hitler had luck — a great deal. He inherited policies which began to lift the German economy from the swamp of recession and unemployment. Much of his support, much of his acceptance, sprang from the success of policies which he would never have had the wit to institute, yet no one was quicker than he in realizing their value. But economic success does not cast the spell on a nation which Hitler cast on Germany. He was a great orator who could play on the whole range of feeling from earthy humor, soap-opera sentiment, fierce patriotism, to blistering hate and lust for revenge. And with these outstanding oratorical powers went a keen sense of theater. Never in the whole history of Western Europe had politics been so theatrically stage-managed as at the Nuremberg rallies: unbelievable spectacles of precise and rigid organization. By such methods Hitler won the devotion of millions of his subjects, a devotion akin to hysterical fanaticism, and, alas, bred a willless terror in the hearts of his enemies and opponents. Yet, alongside this was also great incompetence on Hitler's part — a failure to mobilize the full resources of his country in war; strategic and tactical errors of megalomanic magnitude; misjudgment after misjudgment about people, about events. Norman Stone never overestimates Hitler or his henchmen. He is as alive to their inadequacies as he is to their strengths.

This short life of Hitler by Norman Stone is a masterpiece of analysis, both of Hitler's personal character and of his achievement. There will be endless books about Hitler, as there are about Napoleon — there is never likely to be another which views Hitler and his Reich with such a steady, ironic eye.

J. H. Plumb

25 April 1979

Preface

IN 1945, Hitler appeared to the world as a terrifying figure: a man of immense power and cruelty. It took the world six years of war, and fifty million casualties, to be rid of him. When he died, Russian tanks were only a few hundred yards from the vast Chancellery in Berlin, from where Hitler had dominated the world's affairs. Those of his colleagues who survived were rounded up and tried at Nuremberg for crimes against humanity.

In the last twenty years or so, historical research has somewhat altered the wartime picture of Hitler and nazism. Many beliefs, firmly held at the time, turned out to be misleading. Hitler was not born poor; he was never a house painter; he fought very courageously in the First World War. He did not "seize" power in 1933, but obtained it by means that were at least as constitutional as those that had kept his three predecessors in office. He probably was not responsible for the burning of the Reichstag in 1933. He did not rearm Germany on anything like the scale that people imagined. He was associated with Germany's economic recovery from a devastating depression, but that recovery had nothing much to do with rearmament. He did not plan for war with the western Powers in 1939, or even at any later date. His outstanding military achievements were generally improvisations, and sometimes (as with the bombing of open cities) he was wrongly blamed. I have tried, in this work, to set out the facts of the "revised" Hitler in a relatively brief space. I cannot hope to rival the works of Alan Bullock or Joachim Fest, but this book is based on a wide variety of sources, and I am especially grateful to the German Historical Institute in London for letting me have access to recent monographic literature, not all of which (to my regret) I have been able to mention here.

I should like to acknowledge the help I have had in Cambridge from Jack Plumb and Jack Gallagher, who read the manuscript for me. I have also learned a great deal from discussion with colleagues. It was the late C. W. Guilleband who first fired my interest in Hitler's economic system, and I have had help, in various ways, from Harold James, Simon Schama, Richard Sheldon, Alice Teich, and Joachim Whaley. I owe a very great deal to Richard Overy, whose work on economic and military themes promises to be a contribution of the highest value to scholarship. The History Department of the University of Sidney gave me a warm welcome when I spent the summer of 1978 there, and greatly helped me to clarify my ideas. Finally, I should like to acknowledge my debt to the Wolfson Foundation, for the considerable encouragement it has given me.

NORMAN STONE
Trinity College, Cambridge

Part I

The Road to Power:
1889–1933

1

The Making of a Nazi

"IMAGINARY EVIL is romantic and varied," wrote Simone Weil, "but evil in reality is gloomy and monotonous, barren and boring." To outsiders, Adolf Hitler was a figure of either heroic creativity or satanic destructiveness. But to people who saw him close-to, he was prosaic. While he ruled Germany, and fought for the mastery of the world, his private affairs were so empty that almost nothing can be said about them. He had no interest in love affairs, friendships, religion, intellectual development, or even, beyond a mundane level, money. He did not want a family; his recreations — travel, Westerns, the state of his health, and the sound of his own voice — were boring. He could be kind to secretaries, children, animals, and he had some loyalty toward subordinates. No one who knew him as a man could quite equate what they saw with the realities of Hitler's Germany. And some of his staff assert, even now, that for years Hitler did not even know what was being done to the Jews during the war in his name. Hitler's life was reserved for public, not private, matters. He lived for power. He transferred all of his deep emotions to the harsh technologies of politics and war, machinery and architecture. "The masses," he said, "are my bride."

How does a man become inhuman? Later on, Hitler liked to represent himself as a victim of circumstance who had struggled his lonely way from a very humble base. "It must be quite unique in history for someone like me to have got so far," he mused in 1939. But Hitler's family was not badly off. His father was a senior customs official of the Hapsburg monarchy, who kept a family of five children in comfortable middle-class style in the provincial capital, Linz. For a time, Adolf Hitler went to a boarding school. Provincialism, not poverty, was his problem.

His father had more to complain about. He had been born the illegitimate son of a housemaid, Anna Schicklgruber, in a poor rural district, and he could not even be sure who his father was. The mother did marry when he was five, and her husband eventually recognized paternity, but the real father appears to have been the supposed father's brother. There is at any rate no foundation for the rumor, still current, that the real father was a Jew in whose household Anna Schicklgruber served. The boy survived his background, worked, and became a respected member of the Linz community. He was fifty-two, and into his third marriage, when Hitler was born, on 20 April 1889 at Braunau, a small town on the Austro-German border where his father was serving at the time. Shortly afterward, he was transferred to Linz, and lived in a large middle-class house. His third wife, Klara, was a close relative some twenty years younger than himself, and a dreary creature who, after stillbirths, bore him two children. Relatively early, Hitler senior retired from his post, cultivated a plot of land, and spent time with mistresses.

Already, these circumstances showed a pattern familiar enough among the Nazis of the 1930s: the remote, often absent, irascible, uniformed father much older than his son; the crushed dormouse of a mother, peering sadly out of photographs; the uneasy social position between the purse-proud provincial middle class and the grasping, uncouth peasant relatives. No doubt Hitler, like so many other Nazis, acquired his perverted idea of masculinity from these surroundings — a world of violence, cruelty, lists, and uniforms; no doubt, too, he felt that, socially, he did not really belong anywhere at all.

Hitler did not make up for this by doing as so many other boys would have done in his circumstances, by working hard and fashioning a world for himself. He did not do well at school and would not submit to academic disciplines. His German was poor, his spelling uneasy. He succeeded only with subjects where his undisciplined fantasy could roam — notably history. He was also a decent draftsman. He failed his examinations, and later rationalized, probably correctly, that he had done it deliberately to avoid following in his father's plodding footsteps.

His father died in 1903, leaving the family tolerably off, and his mother followed, of cancer, in 1907. Hitler inherited enough capital to keep him roughly at the level of a junior schoolteacher, and he did not have to starve — on the contrary, as he grew up, he became a fussy dresser, and indulged his taste for opera. He could pay for his own studies, and he made for the Academy of Fine Arts in Vienna, hoping to study architecture. The academy thought quite highly of him, but competition for places was severe and he was twice rejected in 1907 and 1908.

Like many other young men of his type, he could hardly go back home. He stayed on in Vienna, between 1908 and 1913. He lived hand-to-mouth, doing watercolors that were pretty enough to be sold to tourists. It was a very lonely life, and became all the more isolated as Hitler found relations with women difficult. Existence was sometimes precarious, and Hitler may have done odd jobs from time to time. However, contrary to legends that he later propagated, he was never crushed by poverty, forced to live in a home for tramps, or become a house painter. He did, for a time, live in a hostel that was as close to the world of the tramp as a YMCA hostel would be nowadays. The main question for Hitler at this time was, simply, what to do next?

It sounds harmless enough. But Hitler himself said that his Vienna years were "the most exacting school of my life" and that "I owe it to that period of my life that I grew hard and am still capable of being hard." He was horribly lonely: socially gauche, sexually inexperienced (perhaps even latently homosexual), professionally insecure, and divorced from his roots. Besides, Vienna was a place where the weak could suffer terribly. It was a highly stratified city, filled with immigrants from all over Central Europe, and the lesser fleas bit the little fleas in a true hierarchy of contempt. Public manners reflected the city's nature: operatic gallantry in private, breathtaking rudeness in public. The cobblestones of the place oozed resentment and hatred, despite the still-functioning apparatus of the Hapsburgs and the sentimentality of the cafés.

Hitler here picked up German nationalism. The Germans of the Hapsburg monarchy felt threatened by a Slavic tide; some of them also resented the emancipation of the Jews, who by 1900 occupied a very prominent place in the business and cultural life of Austria. Men without roots and without a solid existence would often find some cause with which to give purpose to their drifting lives. Obsessive, conquering nationalism was an obvious prop for a man uneasy about his own masculinity: if that was the prop Hitler found in it, he was in good company, for Lord Alfred Douglas in England and Prince Eulenburg in Germany also turned into patriots of an extreme, if chair-borne, cast. No doubt, in an earlier period, Hitler would have found this kind of identification in the Hapsburg monarchy itself, with its medieval origins and its glossy aristocracy, or in the Church. But now the Hapsburg monarchy projected only a grandmotherly image — well-meaning, inefficient, toothless — while the days of the masculine image of the Counter-Reformation Church had long passed. In any case, it would have been too easy for Hitler to identify with either institution, and, like so many of his type, he despised whatever accepted him (and, in the end, despised the Germans as well). He transferred his emotional loyalties to German nationalism, the father-image at its most crass, the world of *realpolitik*, militarism, big business, Frederick the Great, and Bismarck. This almost psychotic love of Prussia was far from rare. Large numbers of Nazi leaders (as distinct from voters) came from outside Prussia: most were Austrians, Bavarians, Germans born and educated abroad, like Walter Darré in England and the Argentine, Rudolf Hess from Egypt, Philipp Bouhler from Brazil, Hermann Goering, whose father had lived for many years abroad as German consul in Haiti and then as governor of an African colony, Arthur Rosenberg, Max Erwin von Scheubner-Richter, and others from the Baltic. Men like this could project onto Prussia a romantic image seldom shared by people who lived in the country and knew it better.

Hitler was himself the product of a world that was disintegrating; otherwise his father no doubt would have remained a peasant. He, and a great many German Nationalists, did not appreciate this, and they responded to the disintegration by looking for something to blame. Nationalism needs something to hate; and German Nationalism discovered it in Jews. Although many Jews were themselves nationalist Germans, and although there were many celebrated converts (including, in Austria, Karl Kraus and Gustav Mahler), the impact of the emancipation of the Jews from their ghetto was held in many quarters to be destructive. Did not Jewish intellectuals make discoveries that virtually shattered the cultural world of the Gentile? Marx had destroyed the wholeness of society; Freud destroyed the soul; Schoenberg ruined harmony; Einstein abolished even the straight line. Besides, the Jews were more successful in yellow journalism or in predatory high finance. Hitler hated them, and so did many Viennese, whose elected mayor, Karl Lueger, was publicly, though erratically, anti-Semitic.

But if Vienna had been Hitler's training-ground, he could not bear it for too long. In any case, there was a danger that the Hapsburgs would make him do military service. In 1913, he went to Munich, living much as he had in Vienna, and making himself well liked by his landlord, who remembered him as a neat dresser and a constant reader. The Austrian authorities did catch up with him, and he had to whine at them in order to be excused from military service. The letter survives in which Hitler pleaded to be let off. It was misspelled and grotesquely "correct."

When war broke out in 1914, it was for Hitler a tremendous release, a chance to identify with German Nationalism at last. By chance, his image survives in a photograph taken of a cheering crowd in Munich in those August days. Hitler is ecstatic. He had no need to report for military service in the German army, but he did so at once. The experience of war quite often killed the patriotic emotions of young men. It did not have this effect in Hitler's case. He fought fiercely and received two Iron Crosses. One of his officers said, "Hitler never let us down . . . always volunteering for the worst jobs." In the class-bound army of 1914, he could not, without university education, be promoted to the rank of officer, and he never rose above corporal. He was "the unknown soldier." Toward the end of the war, he was badly hit in a gas attack, which made him temporarily blind. He was evacuated to a hospital in Pomerania. It was there that he heard that the German empire had lost the war and the German emperor his throne in the course of a Red revolution.

Hitler had completely lost his bearings. What could a half-trained, not very talented draftsman do now? He had lost his little private income in the wartime inflation. After Hitler recovered, he stayed on in the army. Its chiefs wanted to retain the good soldiers so that future Red uprisings could be contained. Hitler was sent south, to the Munich area, where such a rising did occur and where a brief Communist experiment took place until it was crushed by the soldiers and by armed bands known as *Freikorps*, recruited from demobilized soldiers, farmers, students, and others. For a time, the Communist government in Munich even had control of some of the army units, and a tale went the rounds that Hitler briefly wore a red brassard. When order was bloodily restored in May, Hitler resumed service and was used by the authorities as an education officer: he was to promote propaganda among the soldiers for the Nationalist, as distinct from the Socialist, cause. He was sent by his superiors to observe the activities of small political groups in the Munich area, and in September 1919 he found himself attending the proceedings of one such, the German Workers' Party. It was the start of his political career, for, once he was launched into it, he left the army in April 1920.

The German Workers' Party was one of a number of tiny political groups that had sprung up in Munich at the end of the war. The city was ideal for minuscule political groups that opposed the Reds: rich men would easily part with money to support anything that would save them, the French discreetly fed funds to any movement that might separate Bavaria from the rest of Germany, and there were endless beer halls with small rooms that could be used for semiconspiratorial gatherings. The German Workers' Party had been set up in January 1919 by a small craftsman, Anton Drexler, and a journalist, Dietrich Harrer. It had emerged from a group known as the People's Committee for a Quick Destruction of England that had been set up during the war, and was itself an offshoot of a rich men's anti-Semitic, nationalist association called the Thule Society, which had met since before the war in Munich's best-known hotel, the Four Seasons. The difficulty in German politics, as such rich men saw it, was that their cause never had sufficient mass backing to make any parliamentary showing. They needed small craftsmen who were also nationalistic and anti-Semitic in order to win votes, and so they supported men like Drexler.

The need became all the more acute in the first months of 1919, when Munich was run by the Reds. Drexler and his like — and there were many such throughout Germany — tried to attract the people by talking the language of Socialism: they would denounce profiteers and talk of taxing land, or even of nationalizing it, to prevent the kind of holding-to-ransom in which farmers had indulged during times of scarcity. Equally, the Drexlers of Germany disliked the international side of Socialism, for they could not understand why objections to German profiteers also ought to involve friendship with foreign proletarians. They wanted, in other words, a "National Socialism." That phrase had been used in German Bohemia long before the First World War, and there was even an impeccably democratic Czech political party with that name. The trouble with such groups in Germany was that, although craftsmen and demobilized soldiers might be attracted to them, ordinary workers remained with the Socialist Party, while the bulk of the lower middle class went on voting for liberal or clerical parties. But conditions in 1919 were such that Drexler could enjoy his brief hour of self-importance.

Hitler sat in on a meeting and listened to a professor argue for the separation of Catholic Bavaria from the rest of Germany, which was mainly run, at this time, by Socialists. Hitler answered him, displaying the oratorical skills that had already made him noticed by his officers. Drexler asked Hitler to join the Party and gave him a membership card marked 555. To make the Party look bigger, Drexler had had membership cards numbered from 501. Hitler was in fact the fifty-fifth member. Hitler had found his true profession. He could denounce the Jews, who, he alleged, had made money from the war, chiefly from the postwar inflation, and he could also attack the Reds, whose leaders were

also, he said, Jews. Germany in the postwar years had so many grievances that Hitler was supplied with speeches ready-made, and his
audiences lapped them up. His oratory was strangely effective. Most
speakers who had the mental ability to keep their thoughts in some kind
of order were also too pompous and academic in their style to have any
mass appeal: they would simply read learned tracts to their audience.
On the other hand, men like Drexler, who were quite uneducated, might
talk the language of the people, but would have nothing much to say in
it. Hitler, educated enough to expound his views coherently, also spoke
a popular language. He could be very funny, in an untranslatable,
wholly German way — especially in his use of cruel mimicry or of
suddenly dropped earthy words. A Hitler speech became something of
an attraction in Munich, and, because people paid to hear him, he was
important for the Party's finances. Between November 1919 and November 1920 he spoke at thirty-one of the forty-eight Party meetings.

Hitler had hit upon his greatest gift, one of superb effectiveness at a
time when people depended, even for their most casual entertainment,
on small gatherings based on the spoken word. What makes an orator?
In Hitler's case, of course, he was helped by the fact that his hearers felt
very hard done by. The German currency had been afflicted with inflation, bad enough in the war years but increasingly terrible thereafter.
People on salaries, without the protection of a trade union or a large
industrial combine, were frequently driven to sell their cherished property to survive. Profiteers made killings, sometimes literally so; French
officers strutted arrogantly through the occupied western border-
country; the despised Poles seized what all Germans regarded as arch-
German territory in the northeast and Silesia. Hitler, by denouncing all
of this, found a cause that immediately inspired his listeners.

But Hitler brought something special to the political oratory of his
time. Like many intensely lonely people, he could talk to a large gathering, where he might be rather tongue-tied and gauche in front of a smaller
one; he saw more, in a crowd, than the sum of its parts and could
identify with its collective existence. Quite soon, he attracted intelligent,
educated people. One of them, Putzi Hanfstaengl, a German who had
attended Harvard, recorded of a Hitler speech: "For innuendo and
irony, I have never heard [him] matched. . . . On this evening he was at
his best. I looked round at the audience. Where was the nondescript
crowd I had seen only an hour before? What was suddenly holding these
people who, on the hopeless incline of the falling mark, were engaged in
a daily struggle to keep themselves within the line of decency? The
hubbub and the mug-clattering had stopped, and they were drinking in

every word. Only a few yards away was a young woman, her eyes
fastened on the speaker. Transfixed as though in some devotional ecstasy, she had ceased to be herself, and was completely under the spell
of Hitler's despotic faith in Germany's future greatness." A strange
blend of the masculine and the feminine emerged from Hitler's oratory:
he could lull, but he could also command; and he had an uncanny gift of
alternating. In time, he became highly skilled: he would practice the
speech beforehand, would write out headings on a dozen sheets of fools-
cap with fifteen words or so on each, and then — unlike his rivals — he
would go in without notes. Before such a speech he would be intensely
nervous for a full hour; after it, his shirt would be soaked, dyed blue
from the running of the color of his jacket. It all worked very well, and
the Party coffers filled. By March 1920 the Party was doing well enough
to outshadow other such groupings elsewhere. To mark the extension of
its links to other parts of Germany, the title "National Socialist" was
added to German Workers' Party on 24 February 1920. Hitler had little
difficulty in formally becoming head of the Party in the summer of
1921.

The Nazis — a nickname that came about from the Party's National
Socialist component — were not interested in parliamentary power, not
even in the local parliament of Bavaria. They existed as a paramilitary
group, and Hitler's aim was to launch a putsch, a violent uprising
against the government of the new, Socialist-dominated Weimar republic
(as it was called from the town where it had been formally established).
Hitler's following consisted to a large extent of former soldiers, and he
went on to recruit allies among the army personnel of the Munich garrison, men who would obviously be useful and who could supply him with
weapons. Colonel Franz Xaver von Epp, last commander of the Guard
Regiment of the King of Bavaria, was one sympathizer; so was Ernst
Röhm, who was on the staff of the commander of the Munich district. A
German air-ace of the First World War, Captain Hermann Goering, who
had powerful connections in society, was soon associated. Some of Hitler's wartime comrades also joined; organizational responsibility was
handed to a former sergeant of his, Max Amann. These men naturally
organized themselves in military style. They brought in others from the
Freikorps soldiery, and in time a "Storm Detachment" — *Sturmabteilung*
or, for short, SA — was set up as a special bodyguard for Hitler. It
acquired a uniform in a roundabout way. A consignment of brown shirts,
destined for the Germans who had fought in East Africa during the First
World War, was left in Austria at the end of the war; a Nazi bought it up
cheaply, and by 1923 the SA uniform consisted of brown shirts, in con-

scious parallel with the black ones with which Mussolini, who had just staged his own putsch in Italy, had dressed his paramilitary following.

There were, in Munich, many other such paramilitary formations. Various *Freikorps* hopefuls and their rich supporters had maintained armed groups for possible use against a left-wing uprising. The army authorities usually sympathized with them. In 1919, the Allies had forced the Germans to limit their army to one hundred thousand men, hardly more than a police force. General von Seeckt, who was in charge of it after 1920, tried to get around this by encouraging the paramilitary movements in Bavaria, which had their own weapons from First World War days. However, in most of the German states at this time there were moderate-Socialist governments, hostile to militarism. It was only in Bavaria, with its large farming, Catholic, and conservative element, that a right-wing regime existed under which the militaristic organizations could flourish. The Bavarian governments, right-wing as they were, could encourage the paramilitary movements against the centralizing, moderate-Socialist governments of the Weimar republic. The mass passions that were aroused, first by Versailles, then by inflation, then by the huge indemnity that the French demanded, and finally by the effort of the French, late in 1922, to enforce their demand for money by occupying western Germany, strained the relationship between Bavaria and Berlin beyond bearing. The result was that decent and honorable Bavarian politicians looked with increasing favor on such valiant and determined upholders of Right as the Bavarian military leagues. These leagues might, and indeed did, indulge in violence. They could plot against, and kill, prominent German statesmen. Still, important Bavarian politicians and policemen felt that the paramilitary leagues could be used, and were prepared to tolerate their activities.

Hitler was not strong enough to upset the Bavarian governments by himself. On the other hand, he disliked some of the other paramilitary leaders, since he regarded them as weak toward the Jews and hopelessly favorable toward the old Bavarian monarchists. He was not, himself, a monarchist; he saw monarchy as an outworn form. After all, he had not lived in vain under the Hapsburgs: in his view, they had betrayed the Germanic cause, since they had tolerated Slavs and Jews, and had failed to use force at the right time. Many of the Bavarian military leagues were, however, monarchist. To Hitler's eyes, they would not bring about any significant change at all — in Munich or Berlin. There was a similar problem with the Church. Hitler had been born a Catholic, but he lost his religious faith early on, retaining only a vague belief in "Providence" without any tiresome New Testament connotations. Some of the Bavarian leagues were strongly Catholic; and the Catholic clergy in Bavaria usually condemned anti-Semitism. Hitler repudiated these leagues. He had already divided with Drexler over the question of collaboration with other leagues and had forced Drexler from power by the middle of 1921. Now he had to face the same problem with other, more powerful figures, among them the leader of Bavaria.

In October 1922 Mussolini took control of Italy after he had staged a "march on Rome" in which his Fascist squads, a paramilitary force much like Hitler's, had seized strategic points in the city. Hitler was inspired by this example and by another contemporaneous one, that of Kemal Atatürk in Turkey. Could he not seize power, as they had done? He imitated Fascist practice: colored shirts to begin with, and then theory, such as it was. Nazism borrowed from fascism its salute, the outstretched arm, which it developed in answer to the Communist salute of the fist clenched in anger. The title *Führer*, betokening a leader of an authoritarian militarized state, was taken from *Duce*, the Italian equivalent. The habit of christening Party rallies came from Italy: thus "Rally of Honor," "Rally of Work," and the like. Later on, a number of Nazism's most characteristic slogans — "One People, One Country, One Leader," for instance — were borrowed from Italy and subsequently passed on to such obscure Fascisms as Duvalier's in Haiti. Mussolini had done what Hitler hoped to do. Only, at this time, Hitler was far from sure of his own capacities for statesmanship: he would rather have acted as standard-bearer for someone else. That someone was General Erich Ludendorff.

Ludendorff had been effective chief of staff of the German army in the First World War, while Hindenburg had been commander in chief (theoretically under the German emperor). Ludendorff, who was among the most prominent right-wing nationalists, thought that he could stage a putsch and lead a German revival. He gravitated to Bavaria, looked around, and found Hitler. At this time, Hitler had still not lost that grotesque respect for authority that had hitherto distinguished him. The vast and grunting Ludendorff, blurting his nationalist banalities in *basso profundo* while wobbling his double chins, was a kind of totem for Hitler, who would endlessly raise himself from his chair, bobbing up and down, saying "Yes, Excellency," "No, Excellency" in the for him unusual role of audience. True, the only thing that Ludendorff had in common with Mussolini was his size. But Hitler thought he had picked a winner, and by 1923, the two were closely collaborating.

Hitler also tried to gain the support of General Hans von Seeckt, the army's commander in Berlin. Here, he had taken on someone different from Ludendorff. Seeckt had a sense for reality, although a rather remote one. He knew that if these excitable Bavarians made trouble, they would excite only a left-wing reaction. In March 1920 a right-wing fanatic from East Prussia, Waldemar Kapp, had organized a military coup in Berlin. It had provoked a general strike, a Communist uprising, and, almost, the end of the German army. Seeckt now had learned his lesson: far more could be achieved for Germany and her army by collaboration with moderate Socialists rather than with firebrands of the Kapp or Hitler type. If they succeeded, well and good. But they must not do so with obvious help from the army authorities in Berlin. Hitler saw Seeckt in Berlin in 1922 and was shown the door: "Herr Hitler, you and I have nothing much more to say to one another."

Hitler was thrown back on the resources of the Bavarian Right, and here he was rather more fortunate. Bavaria was run by men of seemingly impenetrable stupidity and seemingly endless guile. They talked, sometimes, the language of separatism, but did not really want to split Bavaria from Germany; they only wished to have a decent, right-wing government in Berlin. Unfortunately, the Prussian voters had a way of voting for the Left or left-leaning center Parties which, when in power, clamped down upon what the Bavarian statesmen saw as their rights. There were endless quarrels between Berlin and Munich in 1921 and 1922 over the paramilitary forces, over taxes, and over the pursuit of right-wing outlaws. In 1923, the French occupied the main industrial districts of western Germany in an effort to make the Germans pay their war indemnity, or reparations, and the Berlin government proclaimed a state of emergency, in which the army had chief executive power. The Bavarian government in turn proclaimed an emergency, and gave chief executive power to one of its senior bureaucrats, an elderly, stiff, right-wing figure named Baron von Kahr. Kahr's police force, headed by one Seisser, was given extraordinary powers to keep order; at the same time, the role of the local garrison commander, Lossow, grew with the state of emergency proclaimed by the Reich authorities. A "triumvirate" thus came into existence. Hitler, leading his large paramilitary force, hoped to collaborate with this triumvirate to sweep out the Berlin government, and then to take on the French, with Ludendorff as leader.

It was a naive plan. First of all, it failed to take account of Ludendorff's weakness: he had become a figure of fun for most Germans, and in any case he was blamed for losing the war, though some people agreed with him that he had been "stabbed in the back." Furthermore, the three Bavarians carried little weight in Berlin, and Seeckt did not wish to provoke the Left, which, indeed, collaborated quite comfortably with him in 1923. And, finally, Hitler overrated the degree of favor he could expect from Kahr. Kahr really wanted to install a right-wing government in Berlin and was not much interested in Bavarian separatism or in German fascism. He disliked the rowdies around Hitler. Of course, he led Hitler on because he could use the Nazis. But he was not going to be used by them.

At this stage, Hitler, whatever his oratorical gifts, was not a good enough politician. He was still absurdly deferential to men like Ludendorff and Kahr, who were educated, pompous, even grandiose. These men were, after all, the incarnation of the German Nationalism he had worshipped from afar. It took him some time to come to terms with the fact that, in nine cases out of ten, these men were waxworks.

Hitler himself was still hopelessly insecure. He had no money and lived, with a motherly creature, in digs that would have been suitable for a bank clerk. He had abandoned his earlier fussiness, had no dress sense, and appeared in a very strange rig-out that was part waiter, part bandit, and part pimp. He had almost no manners, for, when his upperclass patrons, such as Goering and Hanfstaengl, introduced him to a soirée, he would either sit Byronically silent for hours, in his curious garb, or would blurt out an interminable monologue. Sexually, no one knows what happened. Hanfstaengl thought him "the repressed, masturbatory type." He did have very close relations with Ernst Röhm, the homosexual army captain, and later he was very close to a student named Rudolf Hess, with whom he used the familiar *Du* (which he very seldom otherwise did), who was known in Party circles as "Fräulein Anna," and whose wife complained to Hanfstaengl that, when Hess went to bed, he would wave a divining rod under it and then subject her to a process she described as "fit for a candidate for confirmation." But no one knows what went on inside Hitler's head; and he never revealed anything. He was, however, intensely nervous. He loved Wagner, and had Hanfstaengl play Liszt arrangements of Wagner on the piano. He ate quantities of cake, preferably chocolate cake, with whipped cream, and a chocolate swastika piped on top. It was hardly surprising that Kahr did not consider Hitler dictator material, or that Seeckt should have shown him the door.

Hitler did not help his own cause at all through his exclusiveness. There were many other paramilitary leagues in Munich, but Hitler would not collaborate with them except on his own terms. As a result, he alienated them, as he did Kahr. Kahr wanted Hitler's support, but since Hitler advertised radical, even left-wing, views in so many matters, he would not accept full-scale alliance. He allowed Hitler's movement to go on but did not formally support it. By October 1923, things had reached a crisis. Hitler's supporters, demobilized soldiers for the greater part, pushed for action; the contemporary inflation radicalized many of the ordinarily sober middle class; the arrival of the Stresemann government, in which Socialists appeared to be using Liberals, alerted the right-wing Bavarians. When Gustav Stresemann announced that he would try to end the French occupation by agreeing to pay reparations, much of Bavaria revolted. Was this Hitler's hour? Other problems called for action at once, for, in the late summer, the Nazi newspaper, *Völkischer Beobachter* (roughly, the *German Observer*), had attacked Seeckt, who in turn, by virtue of the state of emergency, instructed the garrison commander in Bavaria, Lossow, to suppress that newspaper. Kahr and Lossow, with Seisser's support, resisted the order, and threatened to make that part of the German army stationed in Bavaria swear an oath to Bavaria alone. The crisis was not resolved by 8 November, the fifth anniversary of the German revolution, and Kahr was due, on that day, to make a speech in the largest beer hall in Munich, *Bürgerbräukeller*, or the Citizens' Beer Hall.

Hitler had determined to force the pace. He would move in, with the SA, and force Kahr and his associates to proclaim the National Revolution to create a right-wing government in Berlin. On the evening of 8 November, Kahr spoke to a large, well-off audience. His speech contained, not the rousing appeals that had been expected, but a selection of well-worn middle-class tunes. At 8:30, Hitler burst in, followed by his men. Dressed in a white shirt, with his medals on, and a medley of garments, he jumped up on the table and fired a shot at the ceiling. He yelled, "The National Revolution has begun." SA men filed in with machine guns, followed by Goering, with epaulets the size of fruit tarts and looking "like Wallenstein on the march." Hitler then "arrested" Kahr and his two associates, and escorted them to a back room.

He spoke to them, and Ludendorff arrived to back him up. Now, he said, was the time to march on Berlin. The three were nonplussed: how could a march on Berlin succeed without the help of the gnomelike Seeckt? But they played along with Hitler's fantasy, and dispersed to their offices, ostensibly to arrange things. In fact they behaved quite differently. They alerted Berlin and Seeckt, and looked to their own local defenses. They did not intend to be slaughtered for Hitler's sake.

Consequently, Hitler and Ludendorff, waiting at the beer hall, heard no news, favorable or otherwise. There had been forays outside the local army buildings and there were reports that the army had joined the insurgents. Next day, 9 November, Hitler decided he would march his men to the center of Munich as a demonstration. He led a column of them, and found a cordon of police. He brushed past them. Then he came to the bridge leading into the Odeonsplatz, near the Bavarian War Memorial. This time, there was another police cordon with orders to fire. No one knows who fired the first shot. In any event, Hitler was fired upon. His associate Scheubner-Richter, marching with him, was killed, and in falling he pulled at Hitler's arm, wrenching it from its socket. Ludendorff marched on, in outrage, daring the police to fire at him. But it was the end of the putsch. Hitler fled to Hanfstaengl's country house, and there was arrested.

Hitler had reached rock bottom; but, paradoxically, he said that 9 November had been "the luckiest day of my life." In the first place, he escaped very lightly indeed. He had, after all, committed high treason. But the court was sympathetic toward him, the patriotic front soldier, and Kahr's evidence could hardly avoid incriminating Kahr himself. The trial was a triumph for Hitler, and his cell was flooded with flowers and gifts from well-wishers. The judges sentenced him to the minimum sentence, five years, and recommended him for early parole. But Hitler had absorbed a more valuable lesson. In a country like Germany armed coups were not likely to succeed. It would be better to try the ballot box, to "defeat democracy with its own weapons," as his lieutenant Goebbels was to say later.

Hitler was carried off to prison late in 1923 to await his trial, and after it he remained, until 24 December 1924, in the fortress of Landsberg. Since his behavior in prison was exemplary, he qualified for early release. He was, in any case, treated far from harshly in prison. He had good communal meals with the other imprisoned Nazis, a Nazi pennant flying from his table. He had as many visitors and books as he wanted. Lack of female company had never bothered Hitler, and, even now, at the age of thirty-five, he may well have been a virgin. It was a kind of midlife sabbatical.

Like most prisoners, Hitler ruminated endlessly over the past. Like a good many of them, he was tempted to write. Rudolf Hess — an intense young man with a tuneless whistle and a tendency toward deep-sounding banalities — was imprisoned with him. He was the perfect foil for Hitler who began to dictate a book to him. Most of the result, *Mein Kampf* ("My Struggle") was written in the Landsberg Fortress, and later published, in two volumes (1925 and 1926) when Hitler was released.

Mein Kampf is not very useful in interpreting Hitler's later policies. Historians have seen in it Hitler's master plan: tomorrow Germany, the day after Europe, and the day after that the world. It was an anti-

Semitic work, certainly, and it demonstrated how much harm the Jews had done to Germany because of their profiteering and their left-wing agitation. It also outlined a foreign policy for Germany: an alliance with Italy and Great Britain and the conquest of an empire at the expense of Soviet Russia. More generally, it tried, in quite a manful way, to establish the relationship between individual and community, and to work out what it was that made small countries like England, Holland, or Prussia emerge from their sandboxes and dominate the world. It saw in race what earlier writers had seen in Protestantism: Jews were a disruptive influence, because they were either pastiche versions of the host culture or destructively rebellious against it. *Mein Kampf* seriously attempted to rationalize the various hatreds fizzling around Germany at the time. Hitler wished to find a new morality, a substitute for the Christian one. Most right-wing Germans believed that they had lost the First World War not (as was usually, and rightly, supposed in the West) because they had been too immoral but because they had been too moral — had not drowned enough women and children by submarine; had not killed Jewish profiteers; had not simply bayoneted all those Slavs who had been associated with Germany in the months after the Treaty of Brest-Litovsk in March 1918; and had not simply shot all the Reds who pushed up wages, caused inflation, ruined the middle class, and then made the kaiser abdicate. *Mein Kampf* flattered such prejudices, dressed them up in turgid philosophical language, and sold quite well. Hitler survived on royalties and journalism in the later 1920s, and the book sold almost three hundred thousand copies before he came to power. Of course it was an absurd work: it was long-winded, self-important, and written in an extraordinarily opaque jargon, though not much more so than other works of sociology. But it cannot be taken as a blueprint for anything save Hitler's royalties. Hitler himself dismissed it as "fantasies from behind bars," said he wished he had never written it, and in 1936 ordered the press not to freely quote from it since it represented the realities of 1924 and had value only as "an historical source."

Hitler was released in 1924, but for some time could not act as a politician. The German states, including, in the end, Bavaria, banned the Nazi Party, and Hitler was also banned from public speaking until 1927. It was true that some Nazis had been elected under other tickets, and indeed a proto-Nazi Party secured one-fifth of the seats in the Bavarian parliament in 1924, but these groups had split into several different, quarreling subgroups, and some of them, notably the ones in the Reichstag, had rejoined the orthodox German conservative movement. Hitler was a derided figure and on the fringes of Weimar politics. Things only

worsened for him after 1925, for the republic became tolerably prosper-
ous, and the voters responded by containing their dissatisfaction and
voting for the republican-minded parties. The election of December
1924 resulted in a slaughter of Nazis, and when Hitler re-formed the
Party in February 1925, it was a small group. The election of May 1928
showed no improvement.

The most notable thing about the period from 1925 until 1928 was
that Hitler imposed his leadership on those Nazis who might have challenged it. In north Germany, there were also National Socialists, and
they were much more inclined toward real socialism than the southern-
ers were. They wanted the private property of the German ex-princes to
be expropriated. Some of them wanted alliance with Bolshevik Russia,
and most of them were quite violently against the great industrialists.
Hitler disliked such policies. He regarded social divisions as irrelevant to
real politics. Besides, he wanted the bosses' influence and money. It
came to a fight in February 1926. Hitler solemnly met the northerners at
Bamberg, on the north-south boundary. He had done his homework and
knew that between the two most prominent northerners, Gregor Strasser
and Josef Goebbels, there was something of a gap. Goebbels was very
ambitious to lead the Party faithful. Hitler astutely flattered Goebbels
and promised him the task of leading the Party in Berlin, as district
leader (or, in the Nazis' kitsch-Germanic word, *Gauleiter*). He also
made sure that his own appearance was impressive: he arrived in a
Mercedes, with brown-shirted guards, whereas the others arrived on
motorcycles. The decisive element was that Hitler had the money,
partly from sympathizers and partly from *Mein Kampf*, whereas Strasser had to rely on coins collected from reluctant workers. Not surprisingly, the northern opposition caved in. Strasser accepted the job of
organizer of Party affairs in Munich and Goebbels ran Berlin. The Party's membership was unimpressive, and in 1927 it could not afford to
hold a rally. But at least it had held together, with an organization that
ran throughout Germany. The elections of May 1928 gave the Party
only 2.5 percent of the vote and a handful of Reichstag seats. But Hitler
could wait, confident that his time would come.

2

The Road to Power

"INSTEAD OF WORKING to take power by force, we must hold our noses and enter the Reichstag against the Catholic and Marxist deputies," said Hitler in 1924. How was he to take power by democratic means, once the voters had repudiated him so overwhelmingly? In 1928, the Nazis had campaigned as a radical party, almost as a left-wing one. Their program had called for controls of interest rates and of capitalism generally; one point even stated that land would be expropriated, a throwback to the days of 1919 and 1920 when almost all of the townsmen in Germany regarded farmers, large and small, as the worst of shameless profiteers. But failure in 1928 convinced Hitler that he would have to try a different method. He would need the money of the respectable; somehow he would have to join with the orthodox German Right, the Nationalist Party led by Alfred Hugenberg, and the Veterans' League, or *Stahlhelm*. He would also have to look for votes in the countryside. Therefore he pushed aside his agrarian program, explaining that he intended only to expropriate land that was "used in an anti-national sense" — meaning Jewish land. Instead, he flattered the peasants and set up an agrarian office. At the same time, he opened respectable quarters in Munich, moving from his cramped and dark apartment in the Thierschstrasse to the opulent Prinz-Regentenstrasse. He also managed to obtain money from industrialists in 1929 to back his propaganda against further reparations payments and to institute "The Brown House" in Munich as Party headquarters. It had a grand staircase, a large committee room with a horseshoe table at which stood sixty armchairs in red morocco, with the Party eagle on the back, and a portrait of Frederick the Great glaring down at proceedings. By now, a strange confidence pervaded the movement. Hess wrote to a friend in 1929: "I am sure of ultimate victory; and then we can proceed to our real task, the conquest of empire."

Adolf Hitler was by now well able to bear the strains, the treacheries, and the hypocrisies of democratic politics. The old putschist had been suppressed; a wily politician took his place. November 1923 had rudely deprived Hitler of the absurd deference he had usually practiced with figures of the Old Order, the generals, the bankers, or the princes. He now could calmly use everyone, as Bismarck had been accused of doing, as if they were knives and forks. He had the measure of these waxworks of the Right: despite their pretentious moralizing, they were as stupid and as egoistic as everyone else. As for the "Marxists," they had obviously degenerated into a band of ideological bankrupts, mouthing yesterday's slogans while defending tomorrow's pension.

Hitler was also able at managing Nazi Party affairs. He appreciated that he must never promote men who might challenge him as Gregor Strasser had done; if he did choose an able man as subordinate, that man must be "marked" by another able man so that their rivalry would absorb them, to Hitler's benefit. But Hitler did not much care for able men. His subordinates, while sometimes energetic enough, were chosen for their obedience, not their intelligence; they were a job lot, whose doings sometimes embarrassed the Party. The Party, as Hess once hysterically but accurately declared to a Party rally, was Hitler, and Hitler was the Party. He was his own Marx, his own Lenin, and his own Stalin rolled into one.

Hitler had also come to terms with his peculiar personality. He was never blown off course for very long by emotional disturbances, in the way that a still-young politician could have been, especially when success exposed him to temptation in the Berlin salons. Many women, including the most devoted *horizontales* in Prussia, attempted Hitler's virtue. When Hanfstaengl asked them how they had fared, they would answer "with a shrug and upraised eyebrows." His only affection was for a half-niece, Geli Raubal. No one knows what passed between them, if anything. The girl continually looked unhappy, and killed herself in September 1931. Hitler was upset for a time. Later, he took up with a wholly nondescript girl called Eva Braun, who looked uncannily like his mother. This relationship had only modest sexual content. According to her letters, Eva Braun did not get much sexual attention from Hitler, and in medical tests on him, he was found to have "only half the usual secretion of testis hormone in the blood, comparable to that of a man serving a long prison sentence." There was not much else in the relationship: Hitler seldom saw Eva Braun, and would send his adjutants out to buy flowers or jewelry for her, when he remembered. The flickerings of homosexuality that had been there before 1925 survived only in Hitler's choice of statuesquely handsome uniformed blond adjutants, "the blond front," as they were called. At any event, in 1929, at the age of forty, Hitler had come to terms with life. He was a very lonely man, but he was prepared to settle for a long romance with power.

Weimar politics began to move in his direction in 1929. Weimar had always been a fair-weather system; and the economic climate became foul in that year. Falling farm prices had already caused agitation among the peasantry; in October, the collapse of the American stock market caused further trouble in the cities. Americans began to withdraw their money from abroad, and, since Germans had borrowed heavily, even a modest withdrawal caused trouble for them. Besides, various countries imposed tariffs on German industrial goods, and unemployment rose in the export industries. A spreading stain of economic hardship afflicted the country that year, and by December there were two million unemployed.

The politicians responded with a mixture of childishness, stupidity, and self-righteousness, and it is not too much to say that the Weimar republic killed itself, leaving Hitler to pick up the pieces. The unemployed needed to be paid, and the fund to take care of this had run dry, because no one had expected so much unemployment. The Socialists wished business to pay more into it, and the businessman's party wanted the workers to pay more. One of the great weaknesses of Weimar politics was that the parties were too dependent, in a supine way, upon their own supporters' narrowest interpretation of their material interest. They might have chosen for themselves the utterance of a supposed leader of a crowd in the revolution of 1848, who was found trailing after his flock, and told inquirers, "I am their leader, I must follow them." The parties certainly produced no inspiring leadership and consequently were strangled by their own grass roots. At the time, the businessmen's party was in uneasy coalition with the Socialists. In March 1930 the government broke up in mutual recrimination. Until Hitler's government of 1933, the country did not have a government based on a Reichstag majority.

In other countries, the fall of a government of Left and Center would have meant the rise of a government of Right and Center. But the

German Right, Hugenberg's Nationalists, although occupying a sixth of the seats, was in no mood to collaborate in keeping the democratic system going. Hugenberg, a great industrialist, joined with others of his like in blaming the great depression upon the excessive wages paid to workers and upon the excessive rights that trade unions enjoyed. These, in turn, he blamed on democracy. If democracy were allowed to collapse, would the Right not then pick up the pieces, as the people came to their senses? The president, the aged Field Marshal Hindenburg, appointed a leader of the Catholic Center Party, Heinrich Brüning, as chancellor, and commissioned him to form a government. But Hugenberg would not accept Brüning's offer. Brüning collected only the middle parties, without Socialists or Nationalists, and his budget was outvoted by them and the Communists in coalition.

The depression worsened, and as world trade contracted, German unemployment rose. As unemployment rose, demand declined and food prices dropped. Farmers complained even more loudly than before, and sacked tax offices. But the crisis did not bring the German parties to a majority coalition, as happened in other countries. Instead, it drove both the Left and the Right into resentful telling of ancient class-war rosaries. Brüning had to find economic salvation with a minority government. He was able to govern by virtue of Article 48 of the constitution, which empowered the president to decree laws in the absence of the Reichstag, if they were urgently needed. The laws would have to be submitted to the Reichstag for approval as soon as it met again. The Article was meant to cover emergencies. Now, it covered almost all current business of any importance. Brüning decreed his budget and, until his resignation in 1932, virtually everything else.

His own aims were more to the Right than to the Left. He wished to restore the monarchy and assert the national cause over reparations and armament, and he probably also felt that trade-union rights were too large. Since the Nationalists would not collaborate with him, he could have his decrees put through only if the Socialists refrained from voting against them. Thus, he could not go too far in a right-wing direction without the risk of upsetting the delicate system of "constructive abstention" that German politics had become. The Brüning system was at bottom quite a simple one: if the Socialists threatened to cause Brüning to fall, then Brüning would threaten to fall. Would he not be replaced by a government of the extreme Right, much more horrible to the Left than himself? To ram this home, he needed more Nazis in the Reichstag, to scare the Left and the orthodox Right into submission.

This combination of follies caused Brüning to dissolve the Reichstag, and to proclaim elections for 14 September 1930. By then, it had become clear that economic distress would give the Nazis a good-sized vote — Hitler himself counted on 60 seats. But economic distress gave the Nazis 107 seats — more than Hitler had candidates. The voters came to Hitler because of another failure by the Nationalists. The votes came mainly from the rural and small country-town districts of Protestant north Germany, which Hitler had been courting since 1928. These areas were almost classically conservative ones, and the Nationalists' failure to hold them showed the weakness of their party's management.

The politics of Main Street are not an agreeable phenomenon. Protestant, rural north Germany was in some ways the bedrock of the country, and it had many virtues. The small-town tradition was behind much praiseworthy corporate pride and effort; small towns like Celle or Greifswalde prided themselves on their universities and their opera houses in a way that had no parallel outside Germany, except possibly in the Low Countries. On the other hand there was an unpleasant smugness and a tendency to blame other people if things went wrong. The depression hit these areas very badly. Farmers took on debts in order to augment their businesses and artisans laid in tools, through debt, for similar reasons. When demand for their goods decreased, and bank charges rose, there was trouble. These pious, thrifty, and industrious people blamed taxes, excessive social legislation, high wages, the Jews in banks, and the Jews on the Left.

The Nationalists did not help them. They too blamed much the same people, but, unhappily, they too could be counted among the Weimar profiteers. The Republic had been persuaded to subsidize aristocratic estates in eastern Germany, and the sums of money spent in this cause — *Osthilfe*, or "Help to the East" — were a notorious scandal. Besides, the noblemen were not very good at public relations; not many Germans were. Finally, the Lutheran clergy could not act as cement for a conservative block in the way that their Catholic counterparts could in the Catholic third of the country. The pastors tended to hobnob with the Junker noblemen or the large proprietors and professional men, whereas priests took an intimate part in the lives of their flocks, and, most of the time, directed their votes toward the Catholic Center Party or its Bavarian pendant. In September 1930 the Nationalists lost half of their vote to the Nazis, the right-wing liberals lost half of theirs, and the new voters coming onto the register seemed to have voted Nazi in large numbers as well. Hitler gained almost one-fifth of the seats.

He achieved this by good propaganda. His men could go to villages and make contact with other ex-servicemen. They would arrange "German Evenings," and pass the plate around (not a tin: they knew their peasant and knew that if donations were not public, then large numbers of buttons would be harvested by the collectors). One or another of the hundred speakers trained at the Party's school would come around; and the speakers would have an easy task. Virtually everyone agreed, in these parts, that taxes, reparations, loss of colonies, profiteering banks, and spendthrift noblemen had caused the depression. The Nazis needed only to say that, again and again, to gain votes. They also offered thrills to the young. Goebbels's newspaper in Berlin had something of the appeal of London's *Private Eye*. The SA, with its brownshirts, offered a welcome diversion. In the towns, it could recruit young men only too anxious to beat up Jews or Reds. Unemployment among youth became serious in 1930, and almost two-thirds of the SA in Berlin and Hamburg were made up of such youthful unemployed.

Hitler, with his 107 Reichstag seats, was approached by Brüning for support. No doubt Brüning calculated that Hitler, like any other small party leader before him, would succumb to the delights of respectability. It was, after all, quite standard, in a multiparty democratic system, for small grumble-parties to emerge, for their leaders to preach universal death and destruction, and for them then to fall apart. They usually had ideological cohesion, no discipline, no hierarchy, and a number of corrupt leaders who would desert the party as soon as riches and office came their way. Brüning dismissed the Nazis as a "feverish phenomenon" and was not much discountenanced when Hitler, who deliberately assumed a humble and hesitant air, said he regretted that he could not let his faithful down by supporting a Brüning government that relied on Socialists.

Throughout 1930 and 1931, the depression worsened. In June, 1931, a run on the central European banking system caused one of the largest German banks, the Danat, to close its doors to clients. Foreigners and Germans alike hastened to take their money out of Germany, and the Reichsbank lost most of its gold reserve that month. At the same time, world trade continued to contract, driving yet more people out of work in the exporting industrial countries; agricultural prices, at world level, fell dramatically, so much so that tariffs were raised in almost all of the European countries with a large farming community to protect. This meant that the unemployed could not even have the benefit of cheap food which had usually accompanied depressions in the past. In Germany, the combination of financial, industrial, agricultural, and diplomatic problems was such that the country's economy went into a terrible downward spiral. By the end of 1931 six million Germans were out of work, a figure which did not decline until 1933, after Hitler's rise to power.

Brüning was left with a fractured Reichstag. However, he was strangely full of confidence. Rather as Hugenberg had done, he hoped that crisis would bring the people and their parties to some kind of sense. He himself had something of a program for the recovery of the German economy. It was not a program that involved expenditure of government money on employing people. On the contrary. Brüning and many like him felt that a powerful cause of the depression had been the featherbedding of labor. Wages were too high and trade unions had been given excessive rights under the law, for wage rates negotiated in Berlin between unions and bosses had to apply throughout Germany, regardless of conditions. The trade unions, by insisting on their legal wages at a time when prices and profits were falling, were doing their best, Brüning thought, to continue the depression. He also believed that the constant budget deficit of the Weimar had undermined people's belief in the currency. He used 'Reparation' really as a pretext for carrying out measures that were dictated by class interest. Unemployment benefits must be cut; and in particular, the state salaries. Virtually all Germans accepted that there were far too many bureaucrats. There had been four hundred thousand before the war, and now there were over nine hundred thousand. The Reichstag had contained a large number of such officials, in all parties, and in 1927 these officials had used their influence to vote themselves salary increases of up to 40 percent.

Brüning issued a series of emergency decrees under which austerity was imposed. State salaries were cut, and cut again, to the level of 1924. Monopolies had their prices cut by 10 percent at the end of 1931. Unemployment benefits were trimmed to a pitiful minimum. Women were dismissed, even from theoretically tenured positions. Wages, too, were attacked, and interest rates rose to a height that was quite absurd for a country in a depression (for some loans, 20 percent). The calculation was that such miseries would stimulate harder working and lower wages; thrift, piety, and morality would come into their own again. The effects of the First World War, which in Brüning's view had caused the workers to expect much too much, would be set aside, and Germany would rise again. Unhappily, the only things that did rise were unemployment and the number of Nazi and Communist supporters. In spring 1932, Brüning was stoned in Breslau. His reaction was: "the east is not ripe for democracy."

The Reichstag played a pitiful role in all of this. No one had a constructive alternative to Brüning's policy or wished to take responsibility for it lest he discredit himself in the eyes of his followers. The Reichstag met less often and the Socialists collaborated with Brüning in voting for these lengthy prorogations so that Brüning could proceed with his emergency decrees. When the Reichstag did assemble, there would be a short debate on the iniquity of the decrees, a vote that would uphold them by a tiny majority, and a motion for prorogation that would also be passed with a tiny majority. In order to obtain these majorities, Brüning would have to go in for lengthy negotiations even with the smallest parties among them: the Bavarian People's Party, demanding its slice of post-office patronage; the Economy Party, demanding its concessions for small business; the German Democratic Party, subsequently known as the State Party, which contrived, in the manner of most liberal parties in the latter stages of their decline, to split the more, the smaller it became. On each occasion, Brüning would produce his tiny majority; and his memoirs have a tone of unshakable self-satisfaction. The Reichstag almost ceased to function, meeting ninety-four times in 1930, forty-one times in 1931, and thirteen times in 1932. In the same period, one hundred nine emergency decrees were passed, as opposed to twenty-nine ordinary laws — laws of a kind that even Nazis and Socialists could combine to put through, such as the furthering of discounts, the noneviction of gardeners from allotments, and the removal of tenure from women in the civil service.

German democracy and even German antidemocrats simply were playing into the Nazis' hands. In 1931 and the first few months of 1932, the Party had the benefit of active, continual opposition. Artisans, students, petty officials, house servants, and farmers deserted their traditional parties (except in the case of Catholics) and joined a Nazi Party that would obviously protect them from the ravages of organized labor and big business. Hitler spoke for the new "middle-class proletariat," men who found their hard-learned skills and their proud virtues at a discount in this time of depression and who had to struggle to appear respectable if they were to have any hope of finding work. By spring 1932, when elections were held in separate German states, the Nazis were taking, on an average, two-fifths of the vote, and in some cases, as in the Protestant north (Schleswig-Holstein, Pomerania, East Prussia), they were capturing over half of it.

It was not that Hitler knew anything much about economics; on the contrary, he merely acted on common sense. To him, both law and economics were pseudosciences in which a narrow-minded, profiteering priesthood could make a meal of concepts that were simple and obvious. He despised a subject that pretended to be a science, yet whose practitioners never agreed about anything. He declared that if profiteering businessmen — Jews — and parasitical Reds — again largely Jews — and piratical foreigners — this time, French — were swept away, then confidence would recur and the economy would move again. Nationalism, in other words, would be the answer: "Always in Germany whenever there was an upsurge of political power, economic conditions would begin to improve, but when economics became the sole point of affairs, the state collapsed." This view had obvious plausibility and was adopted by many men other than Nazis. Hitler preached hatred; and it struck a chord.

Had Brüning's policies worked, the story would have been different. But Brüning merely created more unemployment and distress. By the end of 1931, the businessmen themselves began to turn against him, saying that he was too left-wing. Bankers and industrialists of the great monopolies resented the way in which he decreed that their prices should decline; great agrarians, who, despite extremely severe competition, formed the stupidest and most unworthy group of ostensibly responsible Germans at this time, also added to the crisis by demanding even more help for their vast estates in the east. These interest groups began to think in terms of Hitler; and Hitler began to think in terms of them. They had money; he had votes. A marriage of the two would be fertile. In the autumn of 1931 these men tried, in a ceremony known as the Harzburg front, to "capture" Hitler. They failed; Hitler wanted to be leader, which they would not concede.

The interest groups began to lobby Hindenburg for the dismissal of Brüning. Brüning responded in two ways. First, he paraded his European role: foreigners trusted him and would free Germany from reparations and disarmament if he were in power. He then found a seemingly wonderful device to discredit Hitler and to improve his own position at the same time. It involved the president himself. Hindenburg had been elected in 1925; his term would run out in 1932. If the Reichstag agreed, by a majority of two-thirds, to prolong Hindenburg's term, then there need be no popular election for the old man. Hitler would be placed in an immediate dilemma. If the Nazis voted to prolong Hindenburg's term, they would be perpetuating a regime that they opposed; yet if they voted against him, they would appear to be unpatriotic, and they would also deeply offend the old man. In December 1931, this maneuver was launched, when Brüning publicly challenged Hitler to support the prolongation.

Hitler parried this. He stated to Hindenburg that he had great reverence for him but could not support such a candidacy because it would mean indirect support for Brüning. If Hindenburg were prepared to dismiss an unconstitutional government such as Brüning's, it might be a different matter. Hindenburg was therefore forced into a presidential election; and Hitler decided, after endless hesitation, to oppose the old man. There followed two elections, in March and April 1932, to establish a majority candidate. Hindenburg narrowly missed his majority on the first round, and Hitler took just above 30 percent of the vote. In the second round, lesser candidates dropped out and Hindenburg received a small majority, while Hitler took the generous third that formed the standard Nazi share of the vote from then on. It was characteristic of German politics of the time that Hindenburg, the arch-conservative, had to rely for election on Red support. The Socialist leader, Breitscheid, deliciously explained that Hindenburg's presidency hitherto had been "agreeably disappointing."

Hindenburg was not grateful to Brüning for all of this trouble, and he was not impervious to the pressures of his trusted friends in business or agriculture. Above all, he listened to the army. Now, as the depression continued hopelessly, disorder had hit the streets. Nazis and police, Nazis and Reds fought again and again. A speech by Hitler or Goebbels would be an immediate signal for the town rowdies to launch an attack on each other or passersby. Increasingly, there was a likelihood that the *Reichswehr* would have to keep order, and so its leaders became increasingly involved with the government. Of them, Groener was a supporter of Brüning's, and Brüning made him Minister of the Interior as well as of Defense. In April 1932 Groener responded to the street violence by agreeing with the state ministries that the SA should be banned. Groener had been urged to do this by his own closest colleague and friend, Kurt von Schleicher. But Schleicher knew what the reaction would be. Many officers, and a great many powerful Germans, regarded the SA as a useful paramilitary force to deal with the Reds in the event of civil war. There was a storm of rage, in which even the former Crown Prince wrote to Hindenburg to complain of the ban. Finally, Schleicher performed an act of treachery, and told Hindenburg officially that Groener no longer had the support of the army. Groener had to resign as defense minister. His place was taken by Schleicher, who had Hindenburg's ear and who then thought that he could succeed where others had failed: he would "capture" Hitler.

Hindenburg was persuaded to let Brüning go, refusing to sign, on 30 May, the latest of Brüning's austerity measures. Schleicher proposed a government of the Right, which would have the support of business and agriculture and which would have the courage to take on the trade

After a speech, 1922

Hitler and the faithful

Hitler visits a peasant family in East Prussia

Hitler and traditional Germany

The chancellor and his cabinet

Chancellor Hitler meets industrial bosses

The New Germany

unions by emergency decree. It would also be nationalist in character. He needed a chancellor he could manage; and he hit on an ideal candidate in Franz von Papen, the rich husband of a rich wife, an industrialist with a guards-officer, diplomatic, and racing background. Papen was smooth, silly, and a survivor. Schleicher was reproached for making this choice at a time of national crisis. He replied, accurately, "I need a hat, not a head." Papen's cabinet was almost grotesquely unrepresentative. It contained aristocrats and agrarians; there were not even many businessmen in this "Cabinet of Barons." As befitted a system where "interest groups" were supposedly supreme, these groups themselves split, to a point of political helplessness.

The new cabinet launched propaganda concerning "the new state." It distinguished itself at once by removing the Socialist and Catholic coalition government of Prussia and by replacing it with a Reich-appointed commission headed by Papen himself. The Ministry of the Interior produced preposterously old-fashioned edicts concerning the nature of bathing dress in Baltic resorts. The serious business of the cabinet was to draw Hitler into the support of the High Right. Papen obliged Hitler at once by rescinding the ban on the SA and by promising a new election, in which it was obvious that Hitler's Party would secure its standard two-fifths of the vote. The election occurred at the end of July, in an atmosphere of murderous intensity, not lessened by Papen's lifting of the ban. The Nazis duly had 37.6 percent of the vote, with 230 seats at their disposal. They were by far the largest of parties. Then the negotiating began.

Hitler showed himself to be a master of timing and management. Papen and Schleicher wished to have his votes; they were prepared to let him be vice-chancellor in exchange. Hitler knew that in these circumstances he would be trapped into taking responsibility for a full-scale right-wing program, and he turned the offer down. He demanded full powers as chancellor, together with the backing of Hindenburg's emergency decrees. Papen would not have this, and the negotiations collapsed. Hitler was now determined to oust Papen, and he went over to full-scale opposition, the Nazi press ridiculing Papen and his "moth-eaten eagles," the "monocles" that spoke their nineteenth-century jargon while Germany went bankrupt. Papen produced an emergency decree that set aside the trade unions' legal rights over wage levels. In the Reichstag, Hitler joined with the Communists, the Socialists, and the Catholics in voting it down. On 12 September, he even managed, by sleight of hand, to have Goering, the Reichstag speaker, allow a vote of censure on the Papen government. That vote passed (though it was later ruled inadmissible) by 512 votes to 42. It was by far the largest vote of no-confidence ever passed against a German government, and, at that, one whose chief never once addressed the Reichstag. The Reichstag for a time was dissolved, and new elections were proclaimed for November.

In these elections, held on 6 November, there was no momentous change. True, Hitler's vote did decline, as his more conservative followers expressed their dislike of his failure to support Papen, but the decline, to 196 seats (one-third of the vote) still left the Nazis as the largest party by far. The government's supporters only barely increased in number. Papen's business friends urged him to carry out a constitutional coup and to restrict the suffrage. However, Schleicher, whose army would have had to keep order in such an eventuality, announced that the army could not fend off both Reds and Nazis; a Polish invasion-scare was invented to ram the lesson home. In all of Hindenburg's court, there was then only one man who could carry responsibility for a government based on such a tiny minority: Schleicher. He accordingly took over from Papen on 3 December; once more, Hitler had refused his support.

Schleicher believed that he could build up a bloc, or *Querfront*. In the First World War, the German army had proved adept at collaborating with the trade unions, and had mediated between them and employers. Schleicher put out feelers to the heads of the trade union movement and received, at least initially, a favorable response. He also put in train a program of public works designed to relieve unemployment. Then he tried to split the Nazi Party, to obtain the support of its ostensibly left-wing element, under Gregor Strasser, to whom he offered the vice-chancellorship.

This was, in a way, the most difficult moment that Hitler experienced in Reichstag politics. The Nazis were by nature an extremely divisible party. They recruited their following partly from unemployed workers, partly from conservative-minded peasants, partly from careerist bourgeois. The SA in particular gave Hitler a great deal of trouble, for its rowdies believed that, since they did the street fighting, they should be awarded such money as the Party had. Hitler had had to be very careful in his handling of the SA. In September 1930 it had staged an electoral strike; Hitler had forced out its leader, Pfeffer, and, in the following spring, its chief in East Berlin, Stennes. He had taken over the SA himself and invited Röhm back from Bolivia to lead it. Although he could rely reasonably well on Röhm, he also built up a rival and smaller Party force, the SS, under the grotesquely obedient Heinrich Himmler,

to act as personal guard and as Party elite. Gregor Strasser ran the
Party's organization, and he had a fief all his own. Hitler had again been
very careful in discreetly cultivating, not only the chief Gauleiters, but
especially Gregor Strasser's most trusting deputy, Robert Ley. But in
December 1932 the Party was running out of funds. The elections had
been too much for it. How would this affect Hitler's system of clientage,
on which so much depended? Schleicher's approach to Strasser was,
therefore, a highly dangerous moment.

Confrontation occurred in the Reichstag building on 5 December in
the wake of a defeat: in local elections in Thuringia, one of the areas
where the Nazis had shown their first advances, the Nazi vote had
dropped by 40 percent. Strasser argued that the irresponsibility of the
Party was losing it votes. On 7 December Hitler assembled the Reichstag Party and made a brilliant, emotional address, pleading for more
time. Strasser suddenly found himself friendless, as his closest associates
had already been lined up by Hitler. He went off on a holiday, and Ley
took his place. The Schleicher experiment had failed.

Papen then returned to the scene, leading an intrigue with Hitler that
began at the house of a Nazi sympathizer, the banker Schröder, in
Cologne. Papen's industrialist friends had been terrified at the possibility
of a left-wing government with army support. One after another,
Schacht, the financier, Krupp, Thyssen, Bosch, and Siemens, the industrialists, lobbied Hindenburg and Papen on Hitler's behalf. The industrialists' money began to come his way in quantities greater than before.
Papen was asking what Hitler's terms were. They were the same as
before: the chancellorship, and Hindenburg's backing. Papen wished to
associate the Nationalists, under himself and Hugenberg, with the Nazis
in a coalition which would have some two-fifths of the Reichstag seats.
Hitler agreed. He also agreed that Papen should be vice-chancellor, that
eight of the eleven cabinet ministers should be non-Nazis, that Papen
should accompany him when he saw Hindenburg, and that there should
be a neutral defense minister. Hitler merely wished Goering to be Prussian minister of the interior, and Frick, another Nazi, to be Reich minister of the interior. This time, Papen and Hindenburg agreed. There
were brief rumors of resistance by the army; but on 30 January 1933
Hindenburg appointed Hitler to the chancellorshiip.

Part II

The Leader:
1933–1939

3

Consolidation

"EVERYTHING MUST CHANGE," ran a favorite Nazi slogan. Goebbels announced "the National Revolution" and said, "We have abolished 1789." On the night of Hitler's appointment as chancellor, an ecstatic crowd of Nazis marched in procession, endlessly, by torchlight, in SA uniform, around the government quarter of Berlin and *Unter den Linden*. There was, among Hitler's supporters, a tremendous exultation, a feeling of hope at last. Germany was crying out for leadership, and Hitler offered it, where his predecessors offered only weariness, division, the bewilderment.

But what was "the National Revolution"? No one was at all certain. The phrase itself, like much about nazism, was Italian in origin. In Italy, it was supposed to mean self-assertion abroad, self-sufficiency at home, with the class war abolished for the benefit of all save the profiteers; and parliamentary divisiveness brought to an end. In actual practice, no one knew quite what this would mean. Mussolini had instituted a foreign policy of bullying small states, and a policy in home affairs of transforming parliament into a gramophone. But he himself hardly knew what he was about in economic matters, and the fascist revolution came simply to mean a kind of heavily bureaucratized capitalism, with rickety firms paying what amounted to protection money to fascist bosses, great or small.

Hitler, in February 1933, was a very long way from occupying the position that Mussolini enjoyed in Rome. He was dependent, for the

moment, on Hindenburg's willingness to sign emergency decrees on the
government's behalf. The only way to escape from this dependence
would have been rule through the Reichstag; and yet Hitler felt uncomfortable in such assemblies, despised debate, and hated lawyers. In the
cabinet, the three Nazis — Hitler, Goering, and Frick — were outnumbered by the eight conservatives or nonparty specialists; Hitler
could not even see the president unless the conservative Papen were
there as well. Would the election due in March solve anything? Besides,
there was tension between the army and Hitler's part-time Party militia,
the SA. The army feared, rightly, that the SA leaders would take
over the army and use its officers merely as training personnel for the
millions-strong national militia army that the SA leaders wished to see
instituted. Hitler had to appease the generals' discontent. But he could
hardly afford to run down the SA, for he might, in the event of civil war,
have to depend on it. In economic matters, there was similar tension
between the bosses and radical Nazis, who did not care at all for capitalism.

Not surprisingly, February passed relatively quietly. Hitler went
through his constitutional motions, inappositely dressed in top hat and
frock coat, looking, next to the smooth Papen or the bearlike Hindenburg, uncannily like a seedy waiter. He turned out to be an efficient
chairman of cabinet proceedings, and did his homework before sessions.
He did his best to please the Right. His own understanding of economic
technicalities was not more than could be gleaned from a cursory reading of the business sections of the right-wing press, but his government
was pledged to support agriculture and to impose tariffs. It did so in
February. He also encouraged the generals to think of rearmament.

He met them officially, for the first time, on 3 February, at a dinner in
the residence of their leader, Kurt von Hammerstein. The generals were
not very welcoming and even tended to be rather patronizing to this
lowborn newcomer. Hitler on his side was deferential, and he continued
to be so towards such Prussian archetypes for an astonishingly long
time. He knew of course that they could put him out of power if they
wanted, and he also knew he needed them. He therefore played his cards
carefully. He told them his beliefs, and made them out to be similar to
the generals' own: democracy was no way to run a country, for in
politics, as in the armed forces or business life, "only one man can and
should give the orders." He talked about the economic crisis and said
that it could be solved only if Germany captured markets and sources of
cheap raw materials: therefore there would have to be rearmament and
conscription. This must be kept secret, or the French might try to stop

it, but the preparations for a new army and air force could go ahead. He also promised that the SA would not be built up as a replacement for the army, and that the army would not have to interfere in politics. At the same time, he had nothing to say about restoration of the monarchy, a cause dear to the hearts of some officers. Hitler sometimes encouraged monarchist talk, but he had no intention of limiting his own power by restoring the Hohenzollerns. To foreigners, Hitler talked smoothly about peace and goodwill. German representatives continued to attend the League of Nations and the Disarmament Conference; on one occasion that summer, even Goebbels made an improbable appearance at Geneva. Hitler assured Roosevelt that he knew war would bring "sacrifice out of all proportion to any possible gains."

While Hitler consolidated his weak position in regard to the generals, Goering was quietly going ahead with improvements in the Nazi sphere of influence in civilian matters. Goering had been appointed Prussian minister of the interior and was theoretically under Papen, who was governor of that state. But Papen did not interfere as Goering dismissed fifteen hundred policemen of the formerly socialist-minded Prussian police force, which Goering could do because of his ministerial powers. Outright Nazis, such as Daluege of the SS, could then be moved into prominent positions in the police force, and many police officials then turned their coats, advertising their support for the Nazis. Since Prussia was two-thirds of Germany, the changeover in her police force's allegiance mattered a great deal. Even though some of the other German states, notably Bavaria, still had non-Nazi governments, the Nazis' position in Prussia grew quite strong. What would happen next? Hitler proclaimed, on 5 February, a "Law for the Protection of the German People" which empowered the police to raid Communist headquarters. Perhaps he hoped to provoke the Communists to revolt, so that the Nationalists would give him full power. But the Communists did not respond.

Then came an extraordinary event. On the night of 27 February, the Reichstag went up in flames. A Dutchman, Marinus van der Lubbe, was arrested on the spot; he confessed that he had set fire to the Reichstag because he wished to make some act of resistance. His own sympathies were left-wing, and he said he had acted on his own. Almost no one believed this then, and many even today cannot accept the Reichstag fire as the result of one man's actions. Van der Lubbe was accused by the Nazis of having Communist helpers, some of whom were put on trial in 1933, (but not found guilty). The Communists said that the Nazis must have been involved. Certainly, the Reichstag fire suited Hitler extremely well, for it gave him the excuse he needed to attack the Communists and, eventually, other political groups as well. Next day, an emergency decree proclaimed martial law and banned the Communist Party. Goering's police were augmented at once by fifty thousand SA auxiliaries, and there was widespread talk of a Communist uprising — even in the countryside, peasants stood guard over wells to make sure that they would not be poisoned. Goering slept in the Prussian Ministry of the Interior, and well-known enemies of the Nazis were tracked down.

The Reichstag fire gave Hitler the excuse for which he was looking for a strong, dictatorial government. The Communists therefore argued that he had been responsible for the fire. They alleged that there had been a tunnel from Goering's office to the Reichstag and that it had been used by SA men. There is no evidence that this tunnel was used. On the contrary, there was nothing counterfeit in the reactions of the Nazi leaders to the fire. Hitler arrived that evening, scarlet with excitement and rage, denouncing the Communists — "Now we'll show them! Anyone who gets in our way will be mown down." Goering arrived in a vast camel-hair coat and commanded the firefighting. Putzi Hanfstaengl, who had been the first of the prominent Nazis to know about the fire (he had seen the red glare from his window) had telephoned Hitler to tell him, and was told it was "a beacon from heaven." Van der Lubbe insisted that he had had no assistance, and, though this appeared implausible, there was every chance that he spoke the truth. Huge, ornate, heavily timbered buildings with immense dusty drapes and greasy ventilation shafts had a way of burning down from the smallest of causes. The old British House of Commons had gone in this way; the Vienna Stock Exchange burned down because of a cigarette end. Despite appearances, the Reichstag was a vast piece of kindling, and a single man with paraffin enough to soak curtains and skirting boards could do a great deal of damage, particularly when the cupola collapsed and allowed a draft to sweep the flames on. Accidents like this played a much greater part in Hitler's supposedly planned career than was often allowed for at the time.

The government's emergency measures dominated the election campaign. Propaganda, police, and SA men were everywhere as Hitler launched his campaign with a speech at Königsberg. The result, with 89 percent participation by the voters, was something of a disappointment for Hitler, who received somewhat less than a majority. In the election of 5 March, he took 17,300,000 votes, and needed the Nationalists' 3,100,000 to make up a small majority in the Reichstag. He wanted the new Reichstag to give him authority to govern without reference to it in the current period of economic and political emergency — an "Enabling Act," as it was known. This act was technically in breach of the constitution and could be allowed only if two-thirds of the Reichstag voted for it (which had been done in the early 1920s, though of course in favor of democratically minded governments). Hitler had to woo the middle-class parties, especially the Catholic Center.

The new Reichstag session was formally opened with a propaganda ceremony designed to overpower these middle-class representatives, who were of course nationalistic and in favor of support for agriculture. On 21 March the deputies were taken to the garrison church at Potsdam, the center of Frederick the Great's arch-Prussian regime. Goebbels had been at work to make the ceremony unforgettable. The precincts were swathed with swastikas and black, white, and red bunting, the colors of Bismarck's Reich. Hohenzollern princes were there, as were generals of the First World War in their imperial uniforms. Hitler paid extravagant homage to old Hindenburg, and the two descended, after the ceremony, to the crypt, to stand before the catafalques of Frederick the Great and the Great Elector, and lay wreaths. Had Germany arisen, as the Nazis had promised? Two days later, the new Reichstag had its first and last session, in a disused opera house. The government tabled a five-paragraph bill giving it wide powers. Hitler promised the separate states that he would respect their rights and also informally promised the Catholics' leader, Monsignor Kaas, that the Church's rights in education and worship would be unimpaired — the formal document to this effect did not reach Kaas, then or later. The Socialists' leader, Otto Wels, made a courageous speech in defiance of the government. He was answered by Hitler in a speech that purported to be impromptu, but in fact had been well-prepared. He denounced the Reds for impoverishing everyone and humiliating the nation; he said that their Germany was at an end, and that he had no intention of being dependent upon their support. It was the cruel invective of a Trotsky, consigning his opponents to the rubbish heap of history. When voting occurred, none but the Socialists and the few Communists who had risked appearing dared to vote no. The Catholics and the rest of Brüning's bloc, with few exceptions, voted yes. Oddly enough, those who voted no had bungled, in a way, even here, in their last stand. No law could be passed unless the Reichstag had a quorum; and simple abstention by Hitler's opponents could have prevented it from having one so. But the Catholics' desertion of the parliamentary cause deprived the Socialists of their last hope, and they went down courageously.

Hitler then no longer needed the Reichstag and he was much less dependent upon Hindenburg than before. He also determined to lessen his dependence on his right-wing allies, whom in private he mocked and threatened to outwit. He had gained Hindenburg's confidence so totally that the old man himself told Papen he did not have to be present at such meetings in future. The solid interests of the Right had been met by Hitler's agrarian measures, which had the effect of increasing some food prices by 50 percent. Gradually, Hitler then moved new faces into the cabinet. Goebbels became minister of propaganda, ostensibly to "sell" higher food prices to the public on the grounds that they were needed to protect the peasantry and guarantee food production. After April, there was no formal cabinet voting. Hugenberg was sent as German delegate to the World Economic Conference in London, and there made a fool of himself by demanding the return of Germany's colonies — no doubt because he wished to compete with the Nazis, at home, in nationalist talk. The conference protested, and Hugenberg was forced to resign. He later claimed he had done so in protest of Nazi brutalities. His ministries were split up among Nazis, so that the original Nationalists were then outnumbered. Papen was eased out of his Prussian appointment, with Hitler taking it over in such a way that Goering could run Prussia as Hitler's deputy. Other Nationalists, such as Schwerin at Finance, Eltz von Rübenach at Transportation, and Gürtner at justice, continued, under Hitler, until their deaths or the end of the war.

Hitler then closed down rival political groupings. He had hesitated to do this before he had the Enabling Act. In February, he had said that the Communists could not be banned — "You cannot ban six million people." But, with the SA and the police behind him, he could do just that. In any case, the SA had sometimes jumped far ahead of Hitler. Just after the March election, they had instituted a reign of terror — setting up *ad hoc* camps for political enemies, persecuting individual Jews and Socialists or pacifists. In some west German towns, Nazis invaded the Social Security Offices and cut the hair of long-haired social welfare administrators. The SA had occupied many trade union buildings, and in Bavaria on 9 March they carried their leader, Epp, into the role of Reich governor, supplanting the Catholic government in Munich. Hitler proclaimed 1 May as Nazi Labor Day and at the same time declared the trade unions dissolved: in their place would be a Nazi organization, the Labor Front. The trade unions did not respond to this attack. With seven million people out of work, even the stoutest Red would think twice before risking unemployment. Then, in June and July, other political groups were closed down and sometimes were forced to declare, as they dissolved, that they understood the need for it. In July, the Nationalist Party itself was ended, for by now the monarchist, Nationalist cabinet members were in a minority. There was no resistance. After all, was not Hitler carrying out a large part of the Nationalists' own program, in agricultural support, destruction of working-class organizations, and rearmament? And did he not collaborate with men whom the Nationalists respected, such as Schacht for the Economy, Konstantin von Neurath in the Foreign Ministry, and Rohr von Demmin, a prominent Pomeranian land owner, as secretary of state in the Ministry of Agriculture?

Conservatives had grumbles, not so much against Hitler as against the SA. The 2.5 million men of Röhm's paramilitary force were frequently involved in illegalities that made endless trouble for well-off Germans. There were actions against Jews; an SA boycott of Jewish businesses was organized, with Goebbels's support, on 1 April. Throughout March, SA men had set up temporary prisons in such places as the Vulkan docks in Stettin or the Columbia cinema in Berlin. There, and in cellars throughout the cities, their victims would be beaten up. The minister of justice confessed that every time he met the foreign press he was embarrassed, especially so when even defense lawyers were molested. Hitler liked none of this, but he did not object to a show of force to terrorize his enemies. The trouble was that it also terrorized his friends.

Röhm was forever showing off in front of his horrible boyfriends and boasting of his power. He was ambitious for a great military role. He thought that rearmament should involve use of the SA, as a national militia; the *Reichswehr* officers were only to be trainers. He carried such ideas further and often talked of an egalitarian economic order in which bankers and bosses would have no more glorious a part than generals. The SA did not care for capitalism, unless they were themselves given money by it. As 1933–1934 went ahead, a great many of the SA men felt cheated because their party was invaded by hundreds of thousands of middle-class Germans jumping onto the bandwagon — the "March violets," as they were known, from their adhesion in the immediate postelection period. Bureaucratic jobs were held down by men of this stamp, and many SA men got nowhere, whether in Party or in state employment. Röhm himself, though enjoying an opulent enough existence in his Hollywood-style headquarters, was given no state responsibility; and the attitude of the generals toward him was obvious.

The two sides on occasion came to blows. To Hitler, the SA was still essential; in any case, he could often be intensely loyal to old comrades, and Röhm was a distinguished one. Hitler did not mind the homosexual element — even, in a way, approved of it, because it could make the men better fighters, as "it becomes a sort of *Liebestod*." The SA was, however, an embarrassment with his new friends in the army and banking; it was also a nuisance in terms of foreign policy: the British complained that the SA amounted to an illicit armed force. Early in 1934, a crisis came. Röhm would not be content with the largely ceremonial role he was being forced to take. He sent a memorandum to Hitler, arguing for an SA-dominated militia. Hitler disliked this idea. He was, after all, interested in power and not simply in rewarding his less competent subordinates with state jobs. In any case, he could not see "these knock-kneed SA men" as real soldiers. On 28 February, Hitler held a meeting of army and SA leaders in an effort to have them behave amicably. He offered to both the prospect of a strongly rearmed Germany that would have a place for both parties. Röhm solemnly promised to behave, and there followed a joint lunch, at which "the food was good, and the atmosphere frosty."

This ritual made little difference to Röhm. He went on disparaging Hitler's new friendships, and made out that Hitler was betraying "the Brown Revolution." He referred to Hitler as "that ignorant world-war corporal." Worse, he started to make contact with men of potential opposition, such as General von Schleicher and even the French ambassador, with whom he was seen lunching. Did this mean that Röhm was planning a coup and wished to know what the attitude of the French would be?

Hitler drifted. The whole affair became complicated because it involved a crisscrossing of politics within the Nazi Party. Of course Hitler had learned before 1933 how to deal with such problems: from the beginning he had been good at combining technical and personal interests, dividing the various groups within the Party, and letting them squabble among themselves for his favor. But now he had to deal with such affairs at Reich level, and, since the armed forces were involved, whether the SA, the SS, the police, or the army, such squabbling could be dangerous. In the course of events, Röhm was destroyed by combined factions. In the first place, his subordinates let him down. Viktor Lutze, a prominent lieutenant, reported to Hitler and the generals every word that Röhm said against them. And, even worse, Heinrich Himmler, head of the SS but still nominally subordinate to Röhm, intrigued against him.

This occurred for reasons that reflected the power struggle within the Nazi Party. In March 1933, Himmler had been given very little power—he was named police chief of Munich, with Reinhard Heydrich, of the SS Intelligence Service, as his deputy. This was partly because Röhm did not wish to promote him too far and partly because Goering did not wish to push forward the paramilitary side of the Party. Himmler rose because of a different quarrel: that between Goering, who controlled the Nazi establishment in Prussia (including a nascent secret political police, named "Gestapo"), and Frick, who ran the Reich Ministry of the Interior and who could rule the smaller German states easily enough. These two fought for control of the police and much else. Frick promoted Himmler to head the police force in the smaller states, and in November 1933 he abrogated what remained of the states' autonomy. Prussian Goering would not have Prussia abolished in this way, and he maneuvered, in turn, to keep his Prussian government in existence and to protect the police from Frick's clutches. In this period, what appeared to be changes in administrative routine were in fact important political moves.

The challenge from Röhm brought Goering, Frick, and Himmler into alliance. Goering had already set up a "research office" that carried out espionage on internal enemies. Röhm's telephone was tapped. Himmler saw that Goering was too powerful and he therefore struck a bargain with him. The Prussian government remained in existence (as it did until the end) and yet Himmler was named head of the Gestapo, and, somewhat later, of the entire German police. In this way, the Ministry of the Interior, the police, armed forces, and bureaucracy united against Röhm. Since Hitler took his information from one or other of these, he, not surprisingly, began to believe the tales of SA plotting that were fed to him by Goering, whom he trusted, and Himmler, whom, it appears, he disliked. However, Himmler was too insignificant at this time to be a serious threat to anyone. He was useful: he could undermine the SA from within. The SS, at this time only a few thousand men (including Hitler's own bodyguard), counted as much more correct than the rowdy, pederastic SA.

It was Papen, not anyone more significant, who actually precipitated the crisis. The talk of an SA rising could have gone on forever, with Hitler not quite believing what he was told and Röhm making extravagant gestures of loyalty and affection. But Papen launched things. He and his conservative friends in the *Herrenklub*, the nobles' club in Berlin, had been mulling over the rowdyism and tyranny of "the Brown Revolution." If Hindenburg died, as he was soon likely to do, what would happen? On 17 June, Papen spoke out in public, in a speech at the University of Marburg. He denounced the "confusion of brutality and vitality"; he said, "No nation can live in a condition of permanent revolution from below." There was wild applause. Goebbels had the text of the speech suppressed. Hitler wondered: was this a prelude to some action by the High Right? Were the generals loyal? What was Hinden-burg's view? No one quite knows the whole story of what happened. But Hitler saw the generals in connection with the launching of a battle-ship, the *Deutschland,* and, it seems, on that occasion was promised their support for action against the SA by the SS.

Röhm had promised to behave; at Hitler's request, he had even al-lowed the SA a month's leave and had himself gone south, to a favorite hotel at a Bavarian lakeside resort, Bad Wiessee, with various cronies. From 26 June there were constant reports of SA misdoings; Goering and Himmler fed Hitler with tales that the SA were planning a rising and were stacking arms. In some cases, SA troops were given rather mys-terious orders from above to march about pointlessly; and the tales of arms-stacking originated in similar false evidence from someone or other in a high position. From beginning to end, there was no hard evidence of an SA plot, though Hitler might well have believed what he was told, and in any case might have assumed that the SA would launch a plot some day soon. Although he left the running to others, he ap-peared more and more worried and tense. On 28 June he deliberately left Berlin to attend a Party function in Essen, in the Ruhr. On 29 June he received perturbing information from Berlin and finally, late in the evening, having brooded for hours, he responded to a final alert and jumped up: "I've had enough — I'll make an example of them!"

He telephoned Röhm to arrange a rendezvous the next day to make sure that Röhm would be there. Then he flew to Munich. He arrived in the early hours of the morning, dirty and disheveled, and barked at the two officers who met him, "This is the blackest day of my life." He got to Party headquarters in Munich, at the Brown House, raged at SA commanders he met there, and himself ripped off their badges. Then, with an SS guard, he motored out to Röhm's hotel, forced his way past an astonished proprietress, and moved from bedroom to bedroom, ar-resting the occupants and their sleeping companions. Röhm, who had been alone, was completely taken aback; others tried to reason with the SS men they knew. It was to no avail. They were driven off to the Stadelheim prison in Munich, and later were butchered by SS squads.

This done, Hitler had the code word *Kolibri* ("Hummingbird") flashed to Goering and Himmler in Berlin. There, the SS completed the work of arresting SA leaders, including one who was captured on his honeymoon journey, at Bremerhaven, and who went quietly, laughing all the way, because he thought it was a practical joke by SS rivals. Goering, Himmler, and Goebbels, with the help of the army, had drawn up a list of people to be shot. They included Schleicher, two of Papen's closest associates, perhaps Papen himself, Gottfried Treviranus of the old Reichstag conservative group, Kahr of putsch fame, the Nazi who had sold the Boxheim papers to the socialist press in 1931 — in all, eighty-two names. Most, but not all, were tracked down. Papen showed his usual instinct for survival. The SA men shot in the various prisons sometimes died shouting "Heil Hitler." But tales of a plot went on and Hitler used them to justify what he had done. He himself began to suffer from stomach cramps; he told the Reichstag, "It has been terribly hard for me to part with comrades who fought for years together with me." Hindenburg and the generals were greatly relieved. The "Blood Purge" of 30 June 1934 suited them quite well. That it had happened against worthless rowdies of the SA type meant that it need cause no scandal. But it was a clear sign of what Hitler and the SS were capable of doing; Hitler would be above the rule of law.

4

Hitler and the Third Reich

IN THE SUMMER of 1934, Hitler's power was theoretically unassailable. On 2 August, old Hindenburg at last died. Hitler, without opposition, proclaimed himself president and subsequently also head of the armed forces, which had to swear an oath of personal loyalty to him. In 1944 he took the title "Leader" (*Führer*) as an indication that he saw no difference between his positions as head of the Party and as head of state. All of this was ratified by a plebiscite, conducted in circumstances that allowed a dissenting vote or at least abstention. Out of a possible forty-five million, thirty-nine million voted and over 90 percent voted yes. Obvious reservations have to be made before any conclusion is drawn from such voting. But no one seriously doubted at the time that Hitler had attained a peak of popularity among the Germans that no statesman before him had known. Yet he was demonstrably the most immoral ruler the Germans had had for centuries. What was the link?

The first and most obvious one was that Hitler was associated with economic recovery. In 1933, the German economy appeared to be at rock bottom: a quarter of the labor force unemployed, misery in the great cities, foreign trade collapsing, the National Income lower than at any time since 1890. By 1936, it was possible for a neutral observer in Amsterdam to publish a book titled, *The German Economic Miracle*. By then, unemployment had dwindled to nothing, and two years later there was even a considerable labor shortage. By 1936–1937 the national income had almost doubled, to over seventy million marks. Prices and wages had risen to roughly 7 percent, above their levels of 1932, but production had risen by one-third. This pattern held for the following two years.

There are innumerable qualifications to be made. Some industries did not recover, especially the old-fashioned ones of certain kinds of clothing, such as woollens. There were considerable problems, too, in foreign trade. Hitler did not wish to see foreigners dictate the course of the German economy; in any case, industrialized countries abroad were trying to protect their own industries from imports and, therefore, cut down on imports from Germany. Hitler also reduced imports from foreign countries, for an important part of his economic program was to guarantee employment of Germans by having German industry supply its own goods. This meant that Germany could not earn enough foreign exchange, and so could not buy some foreign goods, especially agricultural ones. Consequently there were shortages and German foreign trade became cumbersome and bureaucratic, with forty thousand paper transactions every day as bureaucrats strove to balance imports against exports. Dutch butter and Danish bacon could not come into the country as before. Against that, however, was the fact that numbers of new consumer goods came onto the market. In the Nazi period, Germany experienced a revolution in transport. She had produced, in 1931, 70,000 motor vehicles to France's 200,000, and by 1938, was producing 340,000 to France's 224,000. By 1939, the idea of a small, ordinary, and cheap motor car for the people, the *Volkswagen*, was close to becoming a reality. Housing, electrical goods, radios, and holidays all reflected the Germans' new prosperity. Germans found work and promotion again. The universities, which had stopped issuing doctorates in 1932 because they had become passports to unemployment, started giving them out again in 1934. The bureaucracy, i.e. non-military government employees, expanded by eight hundred thousand. Above all, industry and public works supplied jobs by the million.

A great many people denied, and still deny, the facts of this economic recovery. Communists had comforted themselves with the thought that Hitler's movement was a last desperate attempt to prop up the capitalist system, and that it would soon collapse as the capitalist crisis continued. Quite reputable commentators, by no means all of them Communist, simply refused to admit during the 1930s and even later that Germany had recovered from the slump. When they were driven into a corner, these commentators argued, and have continued to argue, that Germany's economic recovery was somehow "illegitimate," dependent on jobs artificially created through rearmament. It was said that the German economy became overheated: workers were paid for building weapons so that not enough consumer goods were produced and the prices of those rose dangerously. The most prominent western exponent of this view, T. W. Mason, suggests that Germany was on the brink of a great economic crisis in 1939, and escaped it only through war.

The difficulty here is that Hitler had not really rearmed very much by 1936. The Left said that he did. He too said that he did, at least after 1934. In 1935 he said that he had a stronger air force than the British (he did not) and he also told British visitors he was building submarines. At the end of the decade, he boasted that he had spent ninety billion marks on rearmament. A more exact figure was discovered after the war by Allied economists anxious to look into the effects of the bombing offensive on Germany. Nicholas Káldor and J. K. Galbraith were involved. The results of this investigation were published by one of the American participants, Burton H. Klein, in 1952 and again in 1967, with the title *Germany's Economic Preparation for War*, the findings of which were anticipated by Káldor in the British professional press in 1946. To some extent, they had been anticipated, even before the war, by a very sharp-sighted Cambridge economist, C. W. Guillebaud, in his *The Economic Recovery of Germany* (1939). The message of these writers was simple: Hitler was bluffing. All the stories of the unconquerable might with which Germany faced her western enemies in 1939 and 1940, and her Russian archenemy in 1941, are fables. Germany was inferior to both her western and eastern enemies in everything except aircraft, and there her superiority was slight. She had only a few months' stock of vital raw materials and no plans for a lengthy war effort. If her army won battles it was for quite a simple reason: her enemies' armies were very badly led.

"Up to the spring of 1936," writes Klein, "rearmament was largely a myth." We now know that about ten billion marks were spent in the three years from 1933 to spring 1936, the last of these years accounting for just over three billion. By then, the unemployment crisis was over, the sharpest fall having occurred in 1934. It was only after 1936 that arms spending became truly considerable, with over ten billion marks in 1936–37, again ten billion in 1937–38, and over seventeen billion in 1938–39. The vast bulk of this went to feeding and clothing troops, not to new equipment. Germany was producing only 247 tanks every month, which was less than the French, and only 400 aircraft, which was less than the British. The facts of rearmament are complicated enough without their having to bear irrelevant assertions that rearmament caused economic recovery.

Guillebaud suggested before the war that public spending had accounted for Germany's economic recovery, and there is much to be said for that view. Shortly after coming to power, Hitler decided on a great program of road building and improvement of railways and communal facilities. He simply printed the money and did not bother about the deficit he created. He dressed this up as a "Four Year Plan," in accordance with the phraseology popularized by Stalin, though in reality the two economic systems had little in common. Between 1933 and 1936, almost six billion marks were spent by Reinhardt, the Nazi economist who managed this plan. The vast bulk of the money went on roads and *Autobahnen*. These latter were gigantic, concrete motor roads of which three thousand kilometers were built by 1939. They expressed Hitler's personal style of architecture: monumental and stark. Nazi leaders invoked the examples of the Cheops pyramids and the great highways of the Incas. Hitler went in for solemn inaugural ceremonies. When the figures for Hitler's limited rearmament were known, some suggested that the *Autobahnen* must have had a military purpose. But they did not and when the army was asked what it thought of them, it grumbled that the money would be better spent on railways. It was asked again in 1942 and it tentatively suggested their use as landing strips. (The roads did, in the end, have a military function. When Allied bombing began, some German war industry was shifted to the shelter of the tunnels and the overpasses.) The *Autobahnen* directly employed two hundred thousand, with twenty thousand building firms. The German cement manufacturers naturally voted a resolution of gratitude to Hitler.

Hitler's motor roads stimulated other industries, since the people employed spent their money in turn on some service industry. Besides, the roads stimulated the German motor industry, which was the great success story of the 1930s, and together employed 1.5 million persons. This in turn stimulated electrical industries and did far more to absorb unemployment than any other factor.

This public spending was, it seems, an idea that Hitler had had himself. Previous governments had detested the idea of spending money to keep men in work. It would create a budget deficit, which would undermine the confidence of investors, both at home and abroad. Besides, most commentators thought that it would do little good and hurt the workers' morale. Hitler profited from his ignorance of economics and took a commonsense view. He also profited from the fact that the economics practiced by his predecessors had been a terrible failure; even Papen, and still more Schleicher, had come around to that view and had prepared, in 1932, to support public works, though on an infinitely more modest scale than Hitler. Some people had been worried about the inflationary effects of public spending. Hitler answered them quite simply, at Schacht's instigation, by stressing that both wages and prices could be stopped. Such stops were imposed, though not very harshly, after 1936. Inflation was mainly prevented by saving: the fact was that the Germans would save under Hitler because they had confidence that their savings would not be reduced to nothing or be removed by some left-wing government. Savings in 1936 alone amounted to more than those in five years of Weimar from 1926 to 1931. There was inflation, but it was mild until 1938, and not at all severe even then. Hitler seemingly had stumbled upon modern economics. He thoroughly despised economists who, after throwing up their hands in horror at his ideas, then gave them theoretical expression.

The curious thing was that even though Hitler went in for public spending, he did not greatly increase the budgetary deficit. The recovery of prosperity was so rapid that it wiped out the debt quite quickly because, with prosperity, government revenues went up. The Weimar governments had always been deterred from borrowing from the Reichsbank for public spending because of the legal limitation on Reichsbank lending, which required "first-class" security, not just a state i.o.u. Hitler escaped from this limitation by an ingenious device, which he owed to Schacht, of promoting a fake company and a fake bank; the bonds of the company were backed by certificates representing the value of taxes to be paid in the near future. It was never-never security, but, at least formally, the Reichsbank and private banks had to accept it as "first-class" security and issue good money in return. Schacht, as president of the Reichsbank, like other non-Nazi experts such as the planner, Reinhardt, was invaluable to Hitler at this time.

It is at least arguable that Germany's economic recovery was not only due to public spending. More generally, it occurred because nazism produced a different economic mood. Businesses would take on labor, where previously they had hesitated, because there would be no tiresome trade-union interference; savers would put their money into proper savings institutions instead of hiding it under the bed out of fear of the tax man; people would spend their money instead of nervously putting it away against a rainy day, as the French did for most of the 1930s. It is also arguable that the basis of the economic recovery did not lie with Hitler; that the Brüning policy of pushing down industrial prices and pulling up agricultural ones led, in the long (and very painful) run, to a rationalization of industry. For instance, the price of an automobile fell to 55 percent of its 1925 level in 1932, and the number of vehicle firms from 228 in 1928 to 17 in 1933, with costs as a consequence much lowered. There are strong indications that some sections of agriculture had recovered from the slump even by the autumn of 1932 — enough to pull some branches of industry upward. Brüning always felt aggrieved that no one had given him any credit for the recovery of the 1930s. But whoever was ultimately behind it, it was certainly Hitler who benefited.

Goering had trumpeted, "Guns before Butter"; but even the metaphor was misleading. One of Hitler's unique tricks was to give the Germans a sense of community, of sacrifice, of joint effort, while in fact he also gave them a better life. The 2.5 million members of the Party were indulged in many ways. They could wear uniforms and strut about before their neighbors and colleagues; they were empowered to discipline their fellow men. House porters, waiters, clerks, petty officials, and primary-school teachers could enjoy a sense of Mr. Bumble-like importance as they surveyed their miniature empires. They were flattered for their very vices: anti-Semitism made even "the little man" feel like an aristocrat, or at least the Prussian style of aristocrat. If he happened to be one of the 250,000 part-time members of the SS, he could associate with real aristocrats, who made up 10 percent of its officer corps. It was, "I kick, therefore I am."

Hitler also attracted and encouraged the most tedious kind of woman, of whom he had indeed a tame specimen in Eva Braun. The Nazi Women movement was operated by one Gertrud Scholtz-Klink, "Reich Mother-in-Chief" and pioneer of the liberating slogan, "The German Woman is Knitting Again!" Cranks who disliked makeup, dancing of the modern kind, "decadent art" (that is, the Bauhaus and most German painting of the 1920s), and sexuality of all but the most orthodox kind, flocked to Hitler's banner. He would be photographed, endlessly, with staring, blue-eyed, blond German maidens. He was himself, like many semisexless men, good with children, and that gift too was exploited for propaganda purposes, as was his love of his dog — according to Albert Speer, the only being that inspired human emotion in him. Oddly enough, Hitler himself was not a puritan. He had condoned Röhm's doings, and he closed his eyes to the many marital scandals of senior Nazis, who were understandably only too eager to escape from the Scholtz-Klinks they had usually married. Hitler probably picked up his public puritanism because of its electoral value.

He and Goebbels had always understood the importance of speeches and ceremony. In the 1930s these had unique impact. Every year, in September, there would be Party rallies, several days in length, at Nuremberg. Their climax would be a Hitler speech. A whole district of

Nuremberg was set aside for the rally-complex, which was planned (and to some extent built) on gigantic lines. It would be attended by hundreds of thousands of Party members; spectators in the top reaches of the stadium had to wear special spectacles to see anything at all. It was planned to be larger than the Cheops pyramid. Albert Speer, a young architect whom Hitler had come to know from the building of a new Chancellery in Berlin, was given the task of arranging the lights. The result was a vast cathedral of light. When Hitler appeared to address the enormous crowd, drawn up in ranks before him or seated in the stadium, "there shone upwards from a hidden circle of searchlights behind the grand-stands as many spears of light to the central point above. In this bright light Hitler walked down the steps through the group awaiting him and slowly a procession with him at the head marched across the field to the podium. Thunderous cheers drowned the music of the massed bands playing him in. He ascended the tribune and stood there waiting until there was complete silence. Then suddenly there appeared far in the distance a mass of advancing red color. It was the 25,000 banners of Nazi organizations from all parts of Germany. The color-bearers marched with them across the rear of the brown columns on the field. Then they came forward, six abreast in the narrower lanes, and twenty abreast in the wide center aisle, so there was a great tide of crimson seeping through between solid blocks of brown. Simultaneously, the smaller searchlights along the pillared rim above the grandstands were turned down on the field, lighting up the gilded eagles on the standards, so the flood of red was decked with gold." Then followed a Hitler speech.

These speeches had their effect. Their content was, as ever, negligible. The effect was entirely emotional and virtually untranslatable: "So you have come this day from your little villages, your market towns, your cities, from mines and factories, or leaving the plough, to this city. You come out of the little world of your daily struggle for life, and of your struggle for Germany and for our nation, to experience this feeling for once: Now we are together, we are with Him and He is with Us, and now We are Germany." This rally was also notable for a line from the Scholtz-Klink: "Though our weapon be but the wooden spoon, let it be no less effective."

Behind all this gallivanting was the sinister reality of the police state, the concentration camps, and the exodus of Jews. Hitler had always promised that once he had power he would never let it go. The consequence was a strong police, and a police to control that police.

The police force had always been powerful, even in Weimar Germany, and when Goering took over Prussia, he built it up. He developed a small section of the Prussian State Police that had been set up to deal with political matters and turned it into a "Secret State Police Office," the initials of which subsequently were used to form the word "Gestapo." For a time, Goering had resisted Himmler's attempts to take over the Prussian police; but he gave in by April 1934, and by 1936 Himmler had made himself head of the police throughout Germany as well as head of the SS. He developed both forces, with Hitler's support, to the point where the Gestapo and the SS became much the same thing. In 1939, when war broke out, a Reich Security Office came into existence, which ran the SS, the Gestapo, and the SS Intelligence Service, the SD. The system was run by Himmler and his lieutenant, Heydrich. The Gestapo could at least be challenged by the bureaucracy, but in practice, and even, after 1936, to some extent in theory, the powers of the Gestapo were unchallengeable. The Gauleiters themselves, who by then were responsible for much of the day-to-day administration of the state, complained as they found SD informers at work, even on Party activities. In the 1930s, police power was checked, to some extent, by the Ministry of Justice — thus, for instance, the Communists accused of complicity in the Reichstag fire were found innocent, released, and exiled in 1933 — but by 1936 the legal machine encountered ever more frequent obstacles, and during the war the Gestapo was empowered to arrest again any man whom the courts had freed, to confine him to a camp, and even to kill him without further reference to the courts. It was Himmler's lieutenant Adolf Eichmann who organized much of the official anti-Semitism of Nazi Germany, for he was concerned with the emigration of Jews in the 1930s, and subsequently had charge of the transporting of Jews to death camps in eastern Europe. The whole body grew to considerable proportions by 1939. The "General SS," composed of part-time volunteers, rose from 50,000 to 250,000 in the years of peace; an armed, permanent SS force of divisional strength developed out of Hitler's 120-man bodyguard, and subsequently grew into the armed SS, which maintained almost forty divisions and nearly a million men at the front in 1944; and the "Death's Head units" that ran Hitler's concentration camps amounted to 5,000 men in 1937. Gestapo headquarters in Berlin, which had employed 35 people in 1933, employed 607 in 1935. In addition there were over forty separate Gestapo offices in the provinces as well as the ordinary police forces. During the war, terror grew, to the point where over three million men were involved in "security."

Hitler despised constitutional forms, and although even he objected on occasion to the "Black Plague" of the SS, he was never a serious obstacle to the growth of Himmler's empire. The Nazis, as a prominent diplomat said, "had really no idea as to what a state constitutes." Their Reichstag was a despised, seldom-assembled affair. After 1933 Hitler did not often summon cabinet meetings, and after 1937 he even forbade his constitutional secretary, Lammers, to convoke the cabinet informally, over beer and sandwiches. After 1942 his finance minister, Schwerin von Krosigk, did not see him once. The Nazi state operated through jostlings of private empires — Party, Propaganda Ministry, SS, Four-Year-Plan office, and the like — with no legal prescription for their way of doing things. Their heads had always to appeal for Hitler's authorization before proceeding, and in 1942 Hitler casually had the Reichstag decree that his word should have the force of law. Nazism had come to power because it promised "order" at last. But the order that it brought destroyed anything it touched. When Hitler urgently wished something done, he would have to sidestep the jungle of authorities he had himself created, and he would appoint a man with "full powers" for a particular purpose. In time, such plenipotentiaries became so numerous that they joined the jungle. At every level, offices and personnel increased. By 1939, there were eight hundred thousand more officials than there had been in 1933, even though Hitler owed his rise to power, at least in part, to the resentment of the taxpayer at "luxuriating bureaucracy." That many of these new state employees came from relatively low down in the social scale perhaps constituted some kind of social revolution. If so, as with most revolutions, the National Socialist dream degenerated into gunmen and shiny-bottomed bureaucrats.

At least these men worked with efficiency. The Gestapo of the 1930s and the SS during the war were recruited largely from "outsiders," men who had to prove themselves. Although in the beginning Goering's Gestapo had consisted of professional police officers who had served under the Weimar republic when Himmler took over he ousted them (some later joined the German resistance). They were replaced by men, first from the German countryside, and subsequently from Austria, the country of origin of Kaltenbrunner, Eichmann, Globočnik and many another of the outstanding monsters. These men very often had a uniformed father of one kind or another, and had, like Hitler, a quite exaggerated enthusiasm for the kind of hard, masculine order represented by filing cabinets, acronyms, hierarchies, shiny black uniforms, and Heinrich Himmler. They organized concentration camps with a will.

Hitler had promised before he took power that "heads will roll." The first concentration camps were set up by the auxiliary SA or SS police whom Goering roped in just after Hitler came to power. The word itself was, as usual, borrowed — in this case from an originally English expression; for, during the Boer War, the British had rounded up Boer civilians and housed them in camps to prevent guerrilla warfare. There were complaints from Hitler's allies about the way in which these camps were run, and he strove to regularize the system. Himmler, whose chief aide in this matter was the brutal Theodor Eicke, organized it properly in 1936: there were four camps in 1937, Dachau near Munich, Sachsenhausen, Buchenwald, and, for women, Lichtenburg, and later Ravensbrück in Mecklenburg. When Austria was annexed, Mauthausen and Flossenbürg joined the list. In 1937 they contained thirty-five thousand inmates, guarded by five thousand "Death's Head" men. All opposition was mercilessly crushed by the Gestapo with its informers. Although the Nazi state was associated with German economic recovery, there was always a certain amount of trouble at factory-floor level, and workers who made difficulties would be accused of "Marxism" and imprisoned. From 1933 to 1939, 250,000 persons were imprisoned, on average for three years each, for "political offences." Jews, gypsies, would-be emigrants, and homosexuals were also victims. During the war, arrests ran to fifteen thousand per month, the majority of them for economic offenses of one kind or another. In all, the Nazis arrested three million Germans.

The bulk of Nazi Germany's concentration camps were situated near quarries. Forced labor was used to dig the stone that Hitler needed for his vast building projects — *Autobahnen,* the western defenses, or the grandiose public architecture in which Hitler delighted and some of which was begun in the 1930s. By 1944, the SS had built a huge economic empire, based upon the seven hundred thousand inmates of the concentration camps inside Germany and the millions of Jews, Poles, Russian prisoners of war, and foreign resisters whom the SS put through its camps in Poland. It was an essential part of Hitler's state.

The man behind it all was Heinrich Himmler, who, by 1944, had accumulated a whole string of titles — head of the SS, Minister of the Interior, head of the German Police, and Commissioner for the Furthering of the Germanic Race in the East. Had he ever turned against Hitler, as some of his lieutenants wanted him to do during the war, his power was such that he could easily have overthrown the *Führer*. But Hitler had chosen well. Himmler was, up to the very end, the ultra-useful subordinate, the man to whom all power could be delegated, but who would never use it against his benefactor. His interests lay elsewhere. As the bombs smashed Germany's cities in 1945, as the pride of the Germanic race trekked, in shivering millions with pathetic carts and little bundles of horrible food, away from the frontier march of the East, as the Leader himself degenerated into a broken, raving figure in a concrete shelter far below the ruins of the Reich Chancellery, Himmler could still find time to wonder whether the Japanese alphabet and Japanese skulls did not, perhaps, show some affinity with Nordic equivalents.

Himmler's background was of a kind drearily familiar among Nazi leaders — Bavarian, with a stiff, uniformed father and a Scholtz-Klink of a mother, and a family socially pretentious but materially uneasy. Still, Himmler was such a freak that even this unappetizing pair can be excused of responsibility for warping him, the more so as he had an elder brother who seems to have been decent enough. Himmler did not do very well at school, and was just too young to fight in the First World War. He drifted into the anti-Red militia and in 1923 took a small part in the Hitler putsch because Röhm patronized him and took him in. Himmler had, from the start, a painful sense of order. He carried that housewifely mania of the Nazis to excess. Even as an adolescent, he noted down his every movement to the precise minute. He kept a list of books read, and one, too, of letters and postcards received and sent — down to Christmas cards. Again, he distinguished himself in subterranean intrigue from an early age. At school, he was the archetypal teachers' pet. Later, by heroic though invisible maneuverings, he broke up his brother's engagement. After 1919, he drifted, in the way so many Nazis did. He studied for a time at an agricultural college (and posted home to his mother the dirty washing that accumulated during the week), tried to learn Russian (and even to emigrate as an agricultural colonist), and finally ended up as a straightforward parasite on a divorcée eight years his senior who had a farm. The marriage did not last for very long and soon degenerated into an exchange of letters concerning chicken fodder. Early in the war years, Himmler took up with one of his secretaries, and for a time became quite human.

Throughout all of the horrors, Himmler thought that he was only doing his duty at the behest of his beloved Leader. He hated the sight of blood, and fainted on the only occasion when he saw an execution. Quite bizarrely, he reproved and sometimes even had executed SS men who were involved in corruption or unauthorized brutalities in the various camps. He wished the SS to be super-clean, and he busied himself endlessly with the tiniest details of its corporate life — prescribing how porridge should be consumed in the women's homes, for instance. It would have been utterly foreign to Himmler's nature to stab in the back the man whose creed sanctioned his own ways and turned him, the insignificant, ugly little man, into a paragon of the race. Himmler worshipped Hitler. He stood to attention when the *Führer* telephoned; he told his masseur, who once answered the telephone when Hitler was calling, "You should be proud! Write it down so that you can tell it to your grandchildren!" The most frightening thing about him, as with many other Nazi leaders, including Hitler, was that he never grew up. His whole life was simply the same note, repeated over and over again, with increasing shrillness.

Even so, an important question remains. In the 1930s, the Nazi regime went from bad to worse: more tyranny, more anti-Semitism, and more public and moral disintegration. Yet at the same time Germans were doing better, economically, than they had in the 1920s and certainly in the years of depression. Why did economic success not corrupt the regime, and make it easier to deal with, both by Germans and by other countries? Of course, many of the Nazis did become soft and lazy with success, though they sometimes would pull themselves up with a start and remember that their business was to be tyrannical and hard. But the tenor of the regime, as represented by the SS and the Gestapo, and even by Goebbels's propaganda machine, had degenerated, by 1939, to a point where even foreigners who had sympathized with it in the early 1930s turned completely against it. Hitler himself contains a large part of the answer to this.

Hitler did not become soft with success. He despised, as did Himmler, the fruits of success that other men might have wished for. In monetary matters, he did not go beyond small-town horizons. It was characteristic that he would not accept a salary as chancellor or *Führer* although he charged the Reich large sums of money for the use of his face on its postage stamps. He was not interested in women or in men: his sexual relationships seem to have been very distanced affairs. Although she was never a public figure, Eva Braun was always there after 1934. But the two slept apart, and, according to Speer, no demands at all were made on her after 1936. With the talented, good-looking, and well-mannered Speer, Hitler seems to have had some kind of emotional relationship; similarly, part of his entourage always consisted of ephebes. No deductions can legitimately be drawn from any of this, except that Hitler must have been an intensely lonely man, given to fantasy whenever he was on his own. In Hitler's emotional deep-freeze, the political attitudes of the hayseed middle class at the turn of the century remained alive. Of these, anti-Semitism was by far the most powerful.

Once he was in power, Hitler acted out his fantasy. He became, increasingly, an actor imitating himself. He could work himself up into

rages at will, and then come away, wiping his brow, for all the world like
an actor coming off the stage of a melodrama. Sometimes, foreigners
were completely misled by these outbursts into thinking that "the
Leader" was a maniac: it was widely believed that Hitler chewed the
carpet. But the contemporary accounts of his entourage show that the
whole thing had been staged. Of course he did throw tantrums that were
quite genuine, as a man living with his load of frustration and hatred
well might do. Then he became quite incoherent, repeating the same
phrase over and over again: "I'll build aircraft, aircraft, aircraft, aircraft, and I'll annihilate all my enemies." As the 1930s went by, his
public performances were increasingly self-conscious. He would practice
a piercing gaze in front of the mirror. Apparently spontaneous speeches,
his secretaries told enquirers after the war, would have been very carefully rehearsed beforehand. Hitler would pace up and down, dictating
the speech to a secretary, and, there and then, imitate the gestures he
would use at particular points.

He lived for power, and his image of a man of power dictated his way
of life. The private Hitler was a boring and banal figure — fussily ordering the things on his desk; using three different colors of pencil for his
annotations of documents, depending on which of his capacities he was
adopting (presidential, party leader, or supreme commander); a con-
stipated hypochondriac, constantly washing his hands or bathing twice
daily; learning by heart the serial numbers of his record collection;
eating his cake, or putting seven spoonfuls of sugar into his tea, or
gobbling down his quantities of chocolate; endlessly reading his collection of German westerns (he had the entire set of Karl May), or
watching his Hollywood films of an evening; taking tea with visitors,
knees pressed together, listening to the scraping violins among the
potted plants of the *thé dansant* of the Kaiserhof Hotel; chatting with
the "chauffeureska," the vulgar, and sometimes corrupt, shirt-sleeved
entourage with its horseplay on Bismarck's furniture; indulging his fads
about smoking or vegetarianism; gobbling down his long-overdue lunch
of vegetable stew while laying down the law in that style which is forever
Hitler: "the favorite soup in Greece came from Holstein" or "When
young, I learnt the meaning of history." The only point of any interest in
his private doings was that he was physically brave. He could, for instance, have dental treatment without anesthetic — something that
Himmler could not do.

The "real" Hitler was in fact a figure of fantasy, expressing itself in its
anti-Semitism, its foreign policy, its war, and especially in its architecture. Architecture was the true love of Hitler's life. He related political

greatness to architecture in a very old-fashioned way, though he had also absorbed enough of the contemporary functionalist outlook to appreciate that a government building was a sort of machine for tyrannizing.

And what fantasies! "I am building for eternity, for we are the Last Germany," he said. Speer, appointed in 1937 commissioner for the reconstruction of the Reich's capital, planned a vast central boulevard, a hall to hold 250,000 people. Giesler, another of Hitler's favorite architects, was commissioned to build a Party complex of buildings in Munich, with a road 120 meters broad, and a new opera house. He was also commissioned to reconstruct Linz, and flew to Italy to inspect marble for it, though granite was the favorite material for Hitler, who wished his constructions to last for four thousand years. Hitler took the keenest interest in all of this building and kept a large room full of big models in the Reich Chancellery, which he gloated over. The Reich Chancellery itself was built on lines that were meant to impress: vast size, endless marble, endless approach to Hitler through ranks of heel-clicking, black-clad sentries, to an enormous study that Hitler himself felt dreadfully uncomfortable in using — he preferred to work in the old Chancellery, where he had a much smaller study. Even Hitler's so-called country house, the Berghof at Berchtesgaden, was a building fit for an Ian Fleming villain. Huge slabs of red marble adorned it; looted pictures hung on the walls; there was a vast, thick carpet; a huge fire burning in the grate; oversized arm chairs were placed an uncomfortable distance apart, in such a way that guests would have to half shout their platitudes at each other as the sparks leapt from the fire in the gathering twilight. As a birthday present for Hitler, Martin Bormann had a nearby mountain hollowed out for a teahouse, reached by lift. Hitler was not very appreciative. By 1939, Hitler's architectural fantasies had taken over. There would be armies of slave laborers producing the granite for his new constructions — "things that will take your breath away; it's only thus that we can compete with the ancient Romans" — and the whole thing would provide a proper setting for Germany's greatness. Early in the summer of 1939, Hitler told Speer to have the German eagle on public buildings clutch, not the swastika, but the globe.

Success in humdrum political life merely confirmed Hitler's belief that his fantasies had led him in the right direction. By 1936 he had armed — at least to some extent — without his enemies' interference. He had successfully abandoned the League of Nations and the Disarmament Conference, with all their humbug, in October 1933. He had, above all, secured the prosperity of his country. But Hitler would not stop at that.

In his own way, he was an intellectual. He had a vision of the Germany he wished to create. He felt threatened by foreign powers, and in any case he had always talked of making an empire for Germany at the expense of the East. When things worked out for him, he was all the more convinced he was on the right lines. With every success, anti-Semitism, for instance, worsened. The SS and Gestapo were pliant aides in this. By 1936 the police force had taken in newcomers, anxious to prove themselves. Their way up the ladder would naturally occur at the expense of the Jews, whom their seniors were often too remote or even too decent to persecute systematically. Before 1936 Hitler had had to rely upon the Goerings, Blombergs, and Neuraths. After 1936, he was in increasing partnership with the Himmlers and Eichmanns.

Anti-Semitism in Europe was almost as old as Jewish immigration; it was also, until the Enlightenment, respectable. In modern times, the Jews had become at least semi-assimilated — losing their coherence as a community, but not quite gaining a "native" identity. In Germany, as elsewhere, the six hundred thousand Jews stood out because of their concentration in the cities (one-third of them lived in Berlin) and because of their greater success: they were represented in the professions and in business to a much larger degree than their numbers alone warranted. In the early years of Nazism, anti-Semitism contributed to Hitler's popularity, perhaps the more so as it was, ostensibly, quite modest when compared with the anti-Semitism of, say, interwar Poland. In the early years, Hitler had not much idea what he wished to do with Jews, except deny them access to state service. The short, initial boycott of Jewish businesses was followed by the emigration of prominent Jews (and other opponents of nazism such as Thomas Mann), but there were many protests from quite respectable allies of Hitler, such as Hindenburg, when the Nazis attempted further persecution. Gradually, Jewish civil servants were removed and the numbers of Jewish schoolchildren or students were cut down. It was not until November 1935 that a "Law for the Protection of German Blood and Honor" came about, promulgated at Nuremberg, where some (unsatisfactory) definition of Jewishness was attempted with prohibitions on sexual and other relations between Jews and "Aryans," as the non-Jewish Germans were, absurdly, known.

At this stage, the Jewish organizations themselves proposed patience and acceptance of the status quo; perhaps some leaders of the community were even quite pleased that the faithful were again gathered together as a flock. They advised yes votes in the plebiscites, and some advertised solid German nationalism. Prosperity benefited many, and in any case they could not easily emigrate. The British were much criticized for not allowing more than a small number of Jews into a Palestine that had already turned into a theater of warfare between Arab and ' Jew. But the Americans were no more generous — in the five years up to 1938, they took in fewer Jews than would ordinarily have been admitted in a single year. The only country that offered refuge to as many as one hundred thousand was San Domingo. Even it did so on racial grounds. Its dictator, Rafael Trujillo, admired Hitler (though he was himself slightly negroid) and wished to have his country populated by pure whites. German Jews, then Spanish Republicans in exile, then German war criminals on the run, and, finally, Hungarians of the 1956 uprising found refuge there, while several thousand blacks were slaughtered. It was not until 1938 that other countries admitted Jews generously, the British in particular having a distinguished record from then on. It was an emigration from which they gained much.

The ordinary German people would no doubt have been quite content to leave anti-Semitism at its level of 1934; perhaps many, even Nazis, would have felt more comfortable if it had simply gone away. But they felt more akin to the SS than they did to the persecuted Jews; and the SS would not let up. After Himmler became head of the German police, and after the Eichmanns and Kaltenbrunners had made their way up the Gestapo ladder, official anti-Semitism increased. Hitler had obviously determined to solve the Jewish problem by emigration. Jews would be blackmailed into handing over a quarter or more of their property to the state; if they failed to go, they would face persecution. By 1939, three hundred thousand Jews, broadly speaking the younger section of the community, had emigrated. The final exodus occurred because of "The Night of Broken Glass", *Krlstallnacht*, in November 1938.

In the summer of 1938, the Polish government, in one of its outbursts of anti-Semitism, had decreed that any Polish Jew living abroad would forfeit his Polish citizenship unless he complied with regulations that the government itself would make very difficult. There was a danger that the twenty-five thousand Polish Jews living in Germany would become stateless, and so Hitler decided that they should be expelled. These pathetic families were dumped over the border, and for several weeks the Poles refused to accept them. The son of one such family, Herschel Grynszpan, who lived in Paris, decided to make a protest. He walked into the German embassy and shot a councillor, Ernst vom Rath.

It was a wonderful chance for Goebbels, at that on the anniversary of the Hitler putsch in 1923. He had been looking for some way to restore his prestige, for he had just emerged, at Hitler's insistence, from a stormy affair with a Czech actress, and his marriage had very nearly broken up over it. Hitler, who liked his wife, had treated him coldly. The SA was similarly annoyed at the way it had been left in the cold since 1934. They resolved to demonstrate what good Nazis they were. Goebbels secretly told his lieutenants to mount a pogrom. In the night of 8 November, ninety murders took place, while synagogues and several Jewish houses were burned down; thirty-five thousand Jews were taken to concentration camps for forced emigration, and a huge fine was levied on the Jewish community. This was Goebbels's work; the fact was that Himmler himself disapproved of this kind of primitive behavior, which he thought unworthy of the SS, and it would seem that Hitler ordered a halt to it, because it gave hostages to foreign enemies, quite apart from an enormous bill for the insurance companies. From then on, the Jews of Germany made such efforts as they could to leave, and emigration figures, which had run down after an initial leap in 1933, again increased. And yet, when Hitler's relationship with European powers became tense, he alleged that Jewish machinations were responsible.

5

Arms, Anarchy, and Aggression

AS THE CHARACTER of the Nazi regime worsened, its foreign policy became more aggressive. After 1936, Hitler was on the march — tearing up one piece of Europe after another. He talked the language of war and brandished his weapons in the faces of his opponents. He tricked and lied and denounced solemn promises he had made. What was he after? Historians are at something of a loss as to what he wanted. Hitler never revealed very much of himself, and he told Admiral Raeder, his naval chief, that some of his real intentions would never be known even to his intimates. Historians have constructed theses of great ingenuity on the basis of such evidence as we have — *Mein Kampf*, the Table Talk, i.e. Hitler's recorded wartime conversations, or deductions by Nazi or by foreign observers. There is a farfetched notion, current among historians in Germany, that Hitler even had some kind of concrete plan worked out in the early 1920s, and that he adhered to it from 1933 onward. Hitler himself provided the answer to this conjecture: he often said *Mein Kampf* had been just a prison fantasy and that he wished he had not written it.

Still, from the very beginning, Hitler was clearly an expansionist. He told the generals on the evening he first met them, on 3 February 1933, in Hammerstein's flat, that he could see an answer to Germany's economic problems only in expansion toward the East and "ruthless Germanization of it." That was why he told them to arm. In February 1934, when he addressed the SA and army chiefs together, he said much the same; indeed, he talked of "an aggressive war within eight years." In August 1936 he addressed to Goering a document of which only a few copies were made and in which he argued the case for developing the German economy in such a way that a defensive war could be waged within four years, and an aggressive one within seven. This was also what he told Mussolini, who agreed that it was right.

The economic argumentation behind this made a certain amount of bizarre sense, at least according to the doctrines of the age. The classic imperialist powers, Great Britain and France, had begun to appreciate in the 1930s that imperialism of the direct kind cost more than it gave. This was not how the Germans could view the matter, assuming as they did that loss of their colonies had caused them economic hardship. They assumed that the depression was caused by loss of markets for export; imperialism would give these, together with cheap labor and cheap raw materials, and would enable German goods to compete favorably in other markets. Hitler looked to the spaces of eastern Europe for the answer; even in 1934, when the country had begun to recover economically, he told the generals that he did not believe it would last and that aggressive war for empire was the only answer.

But as the economic recovery got under way, other motives for expansion acquired prominence. Perhaps the first of these was Hitler's own desire to create a great Nazi empire for all time, almost purely for its own sake. His architectural plans became increasingly grandiose, and by 1939 they would have required more granite than Germany, Italy, France, and Scandinavia could have supplied in four years' digging. His new Reich Chancellery was constructed "on such lines that people will believe they are visiting the master of the world." Later, there were visions of enormous trains on outsize railways plying from Silesia to the steppes.

Moreover, by 1936 Hitler was in something of a hurry. Stalin had ostentatiously planned to turn Russia into an industrial giant in two Five Year Plans. No one quite knew what to make of the slaughter and chaos that resulted, but the facts of Russian production, if they were to be believed at all, spelled an unmistakable story. The Soviet Union would be unassailable within a few years, especially so as Stalin was disposing of the Jews who had hitherto operated the Communist system. This was an argument that Hitler put down in his memorandum to Goering: Soviet Russia "with a firm, dictatorially and philosophically based will to attack" faced "an ideologically divided world," and it must be Germany's task to build up her strength sufficiently to defeat Stalin. Hitler abandoned the peasant-based romanticism of the early 1930s, aban-

doned the rugged artisan view of things, and took up technology —
tanks, aircraft, defensive structures, and automobiles. He increasingly
talked the language of rearmament.

There was a further factor to Hitler's dynamism — a personal one.
He himself reached the age of fifty on 20 April 1939 (to tremendous
celebrations in Berlin). He was always something of a fusspot in matters
of health, and in 1935 he began to fear that he had cancer, the disease
that had killed his mother. A polyp, though a benign one, was removed
that year from his larynx. Later, there were other ills — eczema on his
leg, which the doctors could not clear up and which prevented him from
wearing boots until it was treated by Dr. Morell. Hitler often leafed
through medical books and knew a certain amount about the subject. He
explained to the generals in 1939 that an assassin might kill him at any
time, or his health might give out; he wanted to move because otherwise
it would be too late, since everything depended upon him and Mussolini.

Hitler often gave several, quite different, reasons for what he wanted
to do. Which of these was sincerely spoken? We cannot know. But,
whatever the reasoning he advanced, Hitler was undoubtedly, in a general way, committed to expansion, at that, most probably, in Soviet
territory. More generally still, he was committed to success; and the
more successful he became, the less hesitant he was in seeking new
successes. With Napoleon it had been much the same: rather than en-
dure tiresome negotiation and compromise, he would always prefer to
win another battle. Hitler's first task would be to overthrow the Versailles order that had kept the Germans "enslaved," as they thought, in
the 1920s. His next step would be to re-establish the kind of Middle-
European empire, including the western part of Russia, that had, fleet-
ingly, existed in 1918 after the treaty of Brest-Litovsk between imperial
Germany and the Bolsheviks.

He began very cautiously in 1933. The army had only seven divisions
— one hundred thousand men — to the Polish forty and the French
ninety; there was almost no air force. Hitler assured everyone that Germany would be well-behaved. There was an alarm or two over Poland's
attitude: how would she, with so much to lose at the hands of a strong
Germany, respond to a nationalist government? Nothing happened. Hitler grew in confidence. In October 1933, he withdrew from the League
of Nations and the Disarmament Conference, pointing out, not altogether unfairly, that both bodies were merely providing a gloss of morality for the unequal treatment Germany had received since her defeat in
1918. Meanwhile he went ahead with such rearmament as the state of
his finances and the willingness of the generals allowed him — that is to

say, not very much, although by 1935 he exaggerated it in public. The army had its hands full with plans for steady increases in armed strength; and the development of full-scale Great Power force, starting virtually from scratch, was bound to be a lengthy business. The same was true of the *Luftwaffe*, since it took four years for an aircraft to go from drawing board to factory.

In 1934 Hitler's caution included offers of friendship with the British. He had always advertised that he had no quarrel with them. He received Anthony Eden in February, and Eden came away impressed with Hitler's sincerity. It was not until July 1934 that the first serious alarm came up. That month, the Austrian chancellor, Engelbert Dollfuss, was assassinated in the course of a Nazi rising. At that time, most inhabitants of Austria regarded themselves first and foremost as Germans. They had been forbidden, at the end of the First World War, to join Germany because the French did not wish to see Germany increased in size — quite the contrary. When Hitler came to power, Austria split: some Austrians preferred independence to nazism and some wished to join Germany in spite of or because of Hitler. A few even believed in Austria. These few set up a ramshackle government ruling by dictatorial methods. The Nazi hotheads in Austria rose. Hitler seems to have known that they would, but he gave them no positive encouragement. The plot miscarried, and the Austrian police regained control. Europe supposed that Hitler had taken the first step in aggression, and the Italians, who wished to keep Austria as their own satellite, moved troops to the Brenner Pass. Hitler explained that he had been maligned. He sent the ineffable Papen to Vienna as ambassador, to explain German policy. Then things settled down again.

It was not until March 1935 that Hitler even started conscription. The development of an army to train millions during peacetime was a very lengthy and expensive business, swallowing enormous sums in barracks, administration, food, and clothing; the generals themselves quailed at the task and could not imagine that they would have a well-trained force, given that they had only one hundred thousand men to conduct the training. The army leaders were themselves very conservative. Fritsch, who had succeeded the anti-Nazi Hammerstein early in 1934 as head of the army, was no friend to conscription, for he felt that a small, high-quality army would give better results. He was overruled, partly by Hitler and partly by more ambitious officers who wished to absorb the army's leadership in a new, overall structure for the armed forces as a whole. Still, by then there were alarms in the foreign press about German rearmament.

These alarms led to the first of several paper declarations in which the Great Powers grandly announced that they would stand by the postwar settlement. At Italian prompting, a meeting occurred at Stresa in April 1935 in which Great Britain, France, and Italy stood together as in the old days. The "Stresa Front" lasted for barely a few weeks. The Italians had their own ambitions in Africa, attacking Abyssinia a few months later; the British disliked this, and both sides then begged for Hitler's favor. In June, he came to a naval agreement with the British, limiting his own naval strength to roughly one-third of theirs. He himself said, "Politically I see the future only in alliance with the British," and he did not even build the one-third strength he had been allowed.

Hitler did not wish to offend the British by adopting Mussolini's cause. They took the lead in proposing economic sanctions against Italy, as the aggressor in Abyssinia. Hitler, not a member of the League, did not publicly participate in these sanctions, but he did decrease his trade with Italy. He even sent antitank guns to the Abyssinians. He expressed pained surprise at British attacks on him, and he willingly received many leading British public figures to explain his point of view. He did not understand why Churchill made such complaint in the House of Commons.

In March 1936, however, he did take his first aggressive step. Under the terms of the Versailles treaty, Germany undertook not to build defenses in or to garrison the territory of the Rhineland. In this way, the treaty makers had supposed, France would be able to invade Germany whenever she had to. The Germans, and others considered this provision most unfair. They had said so again and again. They had been given no satisfaction, had indeed been reproved for suggesting that there should be a change. Hitler then decided to re-militarize the Rhineland, choosing a moment when Italy was at odds with her former allies and when the French government was weak. This was also the first step that Hitler took virtually on his own, although everyone advised against it. The three service attachés in London sent a joint telegram of warning — the French army would surely march. Blomberg, the war minister, was frankly terrified, knowing that the armed forces were much too weak to resist a French attack. But Hitler gambled, and proved to be triumphantly right. On 7 March, German troops (only two divisions) moved into the Rhineland, receiving a tumultuous welcome. The French deliberated, and did nothing but ask the British what they thought. The British, who privately felt that Hitler was merely "moving into his own back yard," produced somewhat hypocritical reasons for doing nothing, and there the matter ended. Hitler and Italy then were collaborating,

and ideological solidarity helped to cement the relationship. Mussolini
was an even more desperate gambler than Hitler. Privately, he despised
the Germans as a race of pederasts and bullies. But he too wished for
expansion, and Hitler clearly would be a better bet than the western powers, who had their own concerns in the Mediterranean and the Middle
East and who would try to block Italy.

Hitler drew closer to Italy throughout 1936. He had always admired
Mussolini, and copied many of his ways. The Italians were also desperate for economic outlets, which the western powers could no longer
offer. Hitler, with his planned foreign trade, would take Italian agricultural produce at will, if the Italians agreed to take German industrial
goods. And so it proved. Upper-class Italians, however, generally disliked the German connection. Hitler himself had not helped very much
during his official state visit to Venice in 1934, for he had been a
thoroughly inexperienced figure, quite dwarfed by Mussolini (he had
even been reduced, when he could not find the switch for the light in his
room, to standing on a chair to twist the light bulb). But the two powers
were thrown together because of British obstinacy. Their union was
confirmed also by events in Spain. There, in July 1936, civil war broke
out between a group of army officers, who adopted Fascist slogans, and
the Republican government. Mussolini and Hitler made common cause
with the Fascists, while the British and French stood embarrassed on the
sidelines. It was yet another gulf between Italy and the West, and Hitler
profited. In October 1936, Mussolini publicly referred to his arrange-
ment with Germany as "an axis" around which European affairs would
revolve. A year later, a formal pact had been concluded, with Japan,
another anti-British power, on the sidelines.

It was in 1936 that Hitler began to step up the pressure. Hitherto, his
rearmament had been steady and methodical; in mid-1936 he decided
that the time was ripe for change. The British had not responded to his
offers of alliance and the French had made a pact with the Soviet Union.
Hitler then began seriously to prepare for war, though he regarded the
early 1940s as the time for it.

One of the very few documents expounding Hitler's own policy was
his memorandum of August 1936 to Goering, with a copy for the war
minister, Blomberg. It talked of war within four years, and, aggressive
war, if need be, in the early 1940s — a date subsequently agreed with
by Mussolini, though perhaps the agreement had less meaning in his
case than in Hitler's. The impulse for the memorandum arose out of a
crisis in foreign currency. Germany did not have the foreign currency to
pay for both civilian imports, such as the oil cake the Ministry of Agri-

culture wanted, and imports of military importance, such as oil and rubber. This problem was linked with another: how could the country fight a war if it did not have oil and rubber? Substitutes would have to be found. As usual with Hitler, the plan had short-term and long-term benefits, even though it would mean spending more money. Schacht, who disliked planned foreign trade, was not in favor of it, but he was overruled. On 18 October, Goering was empowered to set up a Four Year Plan office, with the usual full powers. He was to encourage development of synthetic rubber (*Buna*) and synthetic oil (obtained as a byproduct of coal) "regardless of cost." He was also to increase Germany's output of steel, if possible by lessening her dependence on Swedish iron ore. The cabinet was told on 4 September that "the Plan is based on the assumption that war with Russia is inevitable. What the Russians have accomplished, so can we."

The trouble was that, in the conditions of the Nazi state, they could not. There was, in the first place, no ideological cohesion: should the state take over or should it merely guide the private producers? Goering sometimes blustered about "Prussian socialism," but he shrank from the complications involved in nationalization, and in any case the army organizers were utterly against interference with capitalism. Goering would thus interfere, but never sufficiently to be effective, especially against producers who merely cooked their books if Goering went too far. Again, there was no agreement between the various ministries. The plan had a Ministerial Council, on which sat Schacht, who disliked inflation, planned foreign trade, rearmament, and excessive interference with the market. It also included Walter Funk, a later Reich Minister for the Economy, a drunken and lachrymose pederast who, in his sober moments, felt that the plan should have been run from his office, but who could do little either for or against it. The services were also represented; but they had their own suppliers, and at a time of scarcity were not inclined to pool their resources. Goering disliked and feared Schacht so much that this council met only once. Finally there was the inevitable Nazi self-indulgence. The various departments were run by Party hacks or former wartime comrades of Goering's. They speedily extended their empires, laying in administrative staff, which rose from fifty-eight to over one thousand in a month, the administrative costs rising from thirty-three thousand marks per month late in 1936 to two million a year later. Theoretically, the plan dictated which quantities of raw materials should go to this or that factory — a matter that the industrialists had already arranged for themselves long before. The task of surveying 180,000 firms in 200 different branches was quite beyond the plan staff, who made one blunder after another. Loeb, who ran the raw-materials department, solved the problem of quotas by agreeing to the demands of everyone, and then sending around a circular arbitrarily cutting these in half when he discovered how much iron was available. The price controller was a helpless victim of market forces.

In any case, no one had any serious intention of restricting civilian industry, and Goering seems not even to have appreciated that no effective arms effort could be mounted until such restriction had been undertaken. Hitler's taxes, though greater in quantity because of prosperity, were in proportion no more onerous than those of Weimar: indeed, where Weimar had taxed inheritances at ten thousand marks and upward, Hitler began with thirty thousand. Manufacturers responded to the civilians' prosperity by producing things that civilians wanted to buy, plan or no plan. The Gauleiters, anxious for popularity and in some cases bought up by local industrialists, did not object. Hence, there was in Germany nothing like the long-term planning for rearmament that the British thought out from 1935 onward. Everything was achieved by the shortest of short-term methods: army contractors delivering goods as before, with the plan an increasing irrelevance.

It worked only because, secretly, it was taken over by the giant industrial combines. I. G. Farben succeeded, after it had moved a large number of its staff into the planning office, in obtaining a virtual monopoly of synthetic fuel production, using the state's powers to grant itself considerable privileges. Even so, by 1938, only two-thirds of the target had been met, at that mainly from plants in existence before 1936. *Buna* rubber was rather more successful; but the effort to extract good steel from the low-quality ores located in the Reich was a failure, even though industrialists were blackmailed into investing heavily in the *Hermann-Goering Werke* to produce the steel in competition with themselves. By the end of 1938, when building labor was diverted to the western defenses, the Four Year Plan's targets became unrealistic. A new "War-Economic Production Program" was announced, but the reality, still, in 1940, lay with separate parts of the services privately arranging contracts with private industrialists. The planning was a complete failure in 1939, and it degenerated into a jumble of highly paid, pompous, do-nothing officials.

There were similar confusions in matters of aircraft production. The pattern here was for Hitler to demand a very great number of planes, and for the *Luftwaffe* planners to produce a more realistic plan providing for fewer than Hitler wanted, and for the producers to produce a third less than the plan dictated. The technical personnel of the Air

Ministry disagreed with the combat personnel, and on neither side was there unanimity, either as to which aircraft were wanted or as to how they should be produced. The *Luftwaffe*, which so terrified foreigners, was in fact something of a paper tiger. In the early period, half of its aircraft were trainer planes or converted civil aircraft. Production of warplanes disrupted things, and no one planned an intense, long-term production process by which resources would be devoted, step by step, to preliminaries, buildings, research, machine-tools, and the like before a single aircraft was produced. On the contrary, the *Luftwaffe* planners ate their seed corn, using resources to produce aircraft at once, whereas these resources could have been better employed to build up processes that would create a great many more aircraft over a somewhat longer term, as the British did. In the summer of 1938, Hitler ordered a five-fold increase in aircraft. Within three months, the air staff whittled down the plan to the levels of early 1938, and actual production was one-third fewer than even they had prescribed. By April 1939, the British were producing more aircraft than the Germans did in 1940. The British target was two thousand per month for March 1940, while Germany attained this level, even in unfulfilled plans, only in the second quarter of 1942.

Hitler's rearmament was, then, a great deal less effective than he himself wanted. Of course, it was difficult to stamp armed forces out of the ground in a bare five or six years unless there was a real wartime emergency. Hitler himself was unwilling to impose real sacrifices, whether through taxation, conscription of labor, or rationing. His lieutenants disagreed as to how the economy should be run and were in any case mostly ignorant; and the services did not agree as to priorities. The *Luftwaffe* in 1939 was far smaller than foreigners thought; the navy had only twenty-two submarines fit for the Atlantic; and, though the generals had done a commendable enough job in training 1.8 million men by 1939, expanding their force from seven divisions in 1933 to thirty-one in 1935 and fifty-two in 1939, they had nothing to compare with the 5 million trained French soldiers. Hitler was in no way ready, in 1939, to face war with anything other than a weak, eastern European country.

This did not make Hitler's foreign policy any more cautious. On the contrary: he proved willing to risk war, even with Great Britain and France. In 1937 his relations with both countries worsened; they feared his ambition and his weaponry; and they resented the methods by which the planning of German foreign trade and the manipulation of the foreign exchange value of the mark sometimes ruined British exports, for their own system prevented them from answering in kind. Their calculation that, with success, the Nazis would become more acceptable members of the European club, had not worked; on the contrary, the tales from Germany unfailingly indicated that Hitler was a wicked man. Hitler said instead that he had no quarrel with the British, and that, as he told Lord Lothian, "another Anglo-German quarrel would mean the departure of both countries from the stage of history." But they distrusted him.

At the same time, Hitler came to a proper understanding with Mussolini, and there were state visits, marked by the usual Fascist spectacles. An anti-Comintern Pact was concluded in November, after Mussolini's visit to Berlin, and the Japanese, who by now were hostile to the British, were associated with it. Hitler and Mussolini now talked, between themselves, of war in the early 1940s. Mussolini told Joachim von Ribbentrop, who had been put in charge of the new, aggressive foreign policy, that "he was tired of imposing independence on Austria." Hitler prepared for a new stage. German foreign policy had become as confused as the rest of the state: the Foreign Ministry, the SS Intelligence Service, and even the military all taking a hand, sometimes in a conflicting sense. The old Foreign Ministry now was to be excluded from important decisions. In Ribbentrop, Hitler had a new foreign minister who would sympathize with the aggressive plans of the Third Reich and who would also appear to be gentlemanly. Ribbentrop, a man of rather uneasy social position who liked to imitate English ways, was, in foreign eyes, a fool and a bore. But in Berlin, he had wormed his way successfully through the Party, setting up an independent office to advise it on foreign affairs. Now, he was to replace the conservative Neurath. Hitler thought he was a new Bismarck. As ambassador in London, he warned Hitler that the British were very hostile. Could that hostility be overruled by a series of *faits accomplis* backed by a force that was more bluff than reality? Hitler and Ribbentrop seem to have imagined as much.

On 5 November Hitler attempted to prod his generals into making a better effort at rearmament. In an affair known as "the Hossbach memorandum," the minutes of this gathering in the Reich Chancellery were taken down by Hitler's army adjutant, Colonel Hossbach. Neurath, Goering, Fritsch, Blomberg, and Raeder were present. Hitler's goal was threefold: to obtain a better effort at rearmament, to give the navy more steel, and to convince the military and their conservative allies of the need for rearmament at an intensive rate, whatever the cost in terms of the inflation so much disliked by Schacht at the Economics Ministry. Hitler delivered a four-hour speech, which he wished to be considered as his "political testament." He said that "for the solution of the German question, all that remains is the way of force"; he suggested the years 1943–1945 as the best time for this. He also suggested that if, in the meantime, France collapsed into civil war (as, in 1936 and 1937, she sometimes seemed likely to do), then the opportunity should be taken to knock out Germany's eastern enemy, Czechoslovakia. This address frightened the army leaders, who were scared of war. They talked among themselves of resistance.

Hitler was casting about for ways of dismissing his hostile critics in the government. Chance came to his rescue. In December, Blomberg married, and Hitler, with Goering, acted as his best man. When his wife moved into the official war minister's residence, she reported her move to the police, in the routine way, and the police had cause to look at her dossier. She had been convicted of posing for pornographic photographs years before. The tale went around that the war minister had married a whore. Hitler, suitably scandalized, had a perfect excuse for asking him to resign, which he duly did late in January. Goering had ambitions to become head of all three services. He therefore set out to discredit Fritsch, who was head of the army; once the Blomberg affair had been launched, Fritsch might as well be dealt with also. Goering, acting with Himmler, showed Hitler a police file in which a well-known homosexual blackmailer had confessed, some years before, that he had had dealings with Fritsch, an elderly bachelor. Fritsch was summoned. When confronted with the evidence, his conduct was such that Hitler believed him guilty, for there was just enough in the story to make it plausible. Fritsch was now pushed into resigning, and even his friends in the army were too dumbfounded by the charge to think of resisting on his behalf. Only much later was Fritsch rehabilitated.

In any case, there were plenty of more amenable generals. One of them, Walter von Brauchitsch, accepted the position of army commander, on condition that the state pay off an inconvenient, grasping wife. To prevent Goering from heading the services and giving priority to the *Luftwaffe*, the generals themselves suggested that Hitler should take over the War Ministry. Again, a very pliant officer, Wilhelm Keitel, came forward to act as chief of staff to Hitler in this capacity. Later, Hitler's side of all this developed into the wartime *Oberkommando der Wehrmacht*, OKW, which ran things on the western front, while Brauchitsch's *Oberkommando des Heeres*, OKH, managed the eastern front. While all of this was proceeding, Hitler quietly dropped a number of prominent conservatives. Schacht went to the Reichsbank as president and Funk took his place at the ministry. Neurath became chief diplomatic adviser, a meaningless role. Several diplomats of the old school were removed and replaced by energetic Nazis. Franz von Papen was one of these diplomats. He had been in Vienna since 1934.

Before Papen was finally dismissed, he came to see Hitler and mentioned that the Austrian chancellor, Kurt von Schuschnigg, wished to see Hitler, with Papen as mediator. Hitler was by now in an expansionist frame of mind and he badly needed some kind of crisis and successful conclusion to distract attention from the Fritsch scandal. He responded to Schuschnigg's appeal, rescinded the recall of Papen as ambassador, and sent him back to Vienna. Unwittingly Schuschnigg had launched the first of the four great crises that led to war in September 1939.

It used to be thought that Hitler had schemed to this end: that he had plotted to annex Austria, then Czechoslovakia, and then Poland, a plan of which hints could be detected in *Mein Kampf*. From the documents available, the story is not so plain. On the contrary, it was sometimes the statesmen of these countries, and politicians or public opinion, that appear to have launched the crises. Thus, for instance, in the Austrian crisis it was Schuschnigg who invited himself to Berchtesgaden and not Hitler who bullied him into coming. On the other hand, Schuschnigg was responding to a situation that came about because Hitler was stepping up pressure in the countries on his borders. Each case provided him with a number of excellent excuses and motives for action of the energetic kind he then wanted.

In each country, there was a large German minority, or, in the case of Austria, an almost wholly German population. And in each, the depression had brought discontent, particularly among the young who responded by deserting the clericalism of their elders and taking up the Nazi cause. In Austria, the clericals, based on the Catholic peasantry, the aristocracy, and some parts of the Catholic middle class, made heavy weather of government. They imprisoned Socialists and Nazis in the same camps and hoped that Italian patronage would deter Hitler from causing trouble. In 1936 there had already been one agreement on the point, in which Schuschnigg had relaxed conditions for the Austrian Nazis in exchange for Hitler's "recognition" of Austria. But the local Nazis made trouble for Schuschnigg, and he could not control them without Hitler's support. He also suspected, not wrongly, that Hitler's SS subordinates were behind much of the agitation; and his economy needed German help. He traveled to Berchtesgaden on 12 February 1938.

Hitler's intentions were clear enough. He told visiting Austrians that he did not wish to take Austria into Germany: Germany had needed fifty years to absorb Bavaria, and would need three times that to absorb Austria. He had in mind an Austrian Nazi state, one in association with Germany. He expected this "evolutionary" solution to happen, though he also encouraged the Austrian Nazis. When Schuschnigg came to see him, the "evolutionary" solution was put forward. Schuschnigg was required to take Austrian Nazis into his government and to release the prisoners. An agreement was offered to him; if he signed, Hitler would again "recognize" Austria. Hitler's diplomatic tactics on this occasion were of a kind he often adopted toward the weak: he blustered and bullied, ostentatiously called for Keitel (though there were no military plans), and, over lunch, ostentatiously discussed the *Luftwaffe* with "my two most brutal-looking generals." Schuschnigg, shaken, signed.

When he went back to Vienna, he repented, and delayed ratification of the new agreement. His president did not like the idea of admitting Nazis into the government and thereby, probably, destroying civilized Austria. Schuschnigg decided to make a gesture of defiance, no doubt with the hope that Mussolini and the western powers would stir. He proclaimed a plebiscite for mid-March: voters were to answer the question, "Do you want a Free, Christian, German Austria." The trouble was that a large number of Austrians, perhaps even a majority, did not want such a thing, if attachment to Germany was the alternative. Germany offered jobs and glory. What did Austria offer in comparison? Schuschnigg therefore put himself in poor moral shape by arranging to rig the plebiscite, doing so with characteristic clumsiness. Only male voters over twenty-five were allowed to vote; only yes answers were printed, the others having to be supplied by the voter; and officials of the government party would register the votes. Hitler stormed at the insult. He decided to use force to install his puppets. On 11 March, Schuschnigg, under German pressure, agreed to cancel the plebiscite, but he did so too late to prevent Hitler from ordering his army to cross the border, after a local Nazi had been persuaded to send a telegram appealing for German help in restoring "constitutional conditions." Hitler sent off an envoy to Mussolini to find out his attitude. The envoy told Hitler by telephone on the night of 11 March that Mussolini fully understood what Hitler was doing. Hitler, sobbing with the relief of tension, gasped, "Tell Mussolini I shall never forget him for this, never, never, never, come what may." He kept that promise.

He himself flew to Munich on 12 March and crossed into Austria. He went to Linz, where he had spent his youth. He did not, at that stage, intend to annex Austria. What turned his head was the extravagant display of enthusiasm that he encountered. The Austrians went wild:

crowds of a size that Vienna had never seen gathered when he visited
that city on 14 March. German tanks, which, because of the relative
absence of military planning for this, did not have enough petrol, simply
drove up to the garages on the way. Hitler declared from the Linz town
hall that he had decided "to return my beloved native country to the
German Reich." It was not until much later that Austrians began to
repent of what they had done.

In the next crisis, German nationalism was again involved. The
Czechoslovakian Republic had been set up in 1918 out of the ruins of
the Hapsburg monarchy. It contained over three million German speakers, usually but inaccurately known as the Sudeten Germans. They had
not wished to join a Czech-run state, and by 1938 three-quarters of
them supported their Nationalist Party, which was run on semi-Nazi
lines. The Austrian affair put them into a state of ungovernable excitement. Hitler would have been delighted had Czechoslovakia broken up
there and then. She was the only democratic state east of the Rhine; she
was allied to France and Russia; her chief area, Bohemia, contained the
only advanced industry east of the Rhine apart from Germany's. Hitler
knew, too, that morally he had a case. The Sudeten Germans had never
been given the self-determination of peoples that the peacemakers of
Versailles had pretended to offer. Many enlightened people in Great
Britain sympathized with them. And it was not only Germany who could
complain of the minority problem in Czechoslovakia. That country also
contained Hungarians who had not been consulted when Slovakia was
attached to the new state; and there were also one hundred thousand
Poles, in an area with valuable mines.

However, Czechoslovakia was a much stronger country than Austria,
and she had allies. Hitler could work on the Sudeten Germans, and his
lieutenants did so, but he could not arrange for a revolt, since the Czechoslovakian police had the situation in hand. Hitler declared on 21 May,
"It is not my intention to destroy Czechoslovakia in the near future
unless provoked." It was the Czechoslovakian president, Eduard Beneš,
who, like Schuschnigg, provided the immediate reason for action. He
claimed, without evidence, that Hitler had mobilized. Hitler had not;
what Beneš was no doubt attempting to do was to alert the western
powers to their duties, and to give himself an excuse for proclaiming
martial law in case the Sudeten Germans attempted an uprising. Hitler
responded and on 30 May produced a military directive to the effect that
he would begin military operations against Czechoslovakia by the beginning of October. Keitel was instructed to have this plan, "Case Green,"
ready. Meanwhile, western defenses were hurriedly built up, artillery

The agrarian romantic

With the workers at Siemensstadt

"This is how a statesman behaves toward the workers"

Ceremonial beginning of work on the first Autobahn, *September 1933*

Hitler at the party's commemoration rally "For Fallen Heroes"

exercises were staged along the Bohemian border, and a French air-force general was given a terrifying (and faked) display of the *Luft-waffe*'s might.

Did Hitler mean war, even if the western powers and Russia intervened to save Czechoslovakia, as the alliance system would have allowed them? No one really knows the answer to this question. Hitler acted as if he meant war, and he terrified his generals with this prospect. Some of them conspired to overthrow him, though the conspiracy did not go beyond talk. On the other hand, there are strong indications that Hitler was bluffing and that he guessed that the western powers would not risk a world war over the question of minority rights in Czechoslovakia. Hitler's armed forces were not at all ready for war. He pretended that they were.

Meanwhile, he increased the tension. He delivered a fiery speech at the Party rally early in September: "I shall not permit, here in the heart of Germany, a second Palestine. The poor Arabs are defenseless and deserted. The Germans in Czechoslovakia are neither defenseless nor deserted." However, the expected Sudeten German uprising fizzled out; even some of the Nationalists there began to have doubts about annexation by Hitler. But, by then, the British wished to end the tension. They hoped to arrive at some understanding with Hitler, some way by which he would return to peaceful paths. Sir Neville Chamberlain, the sixty-nine-year-old British prime minister, flew to meet Hitler at Munich on 15 September and the two men discussed the whole problem. In the Berghof, Hitler spoke quite reasonably, suggesting that he should be given the Sudeten German areas after a plebiscite. Unhappily for the Czechs, these areas included their frontier defenses, but Chamberlain did not believe these were worth an Anglo-German war. He went back to obtain his cabinet's agreement. On 19 September, an Anglo-French plan for the cession of the Sudetenland was presented to the Czechs. Beneš played for time, hoping that the conscience of public opinion in Paris and London would overthrow the two treacherous governments. It took something like an ultimatum for Beneš finally to give way.

Hitler, on his side, wanted more than merely the Sudetenland. He wished to dismember Czechoslovakia, and he received Poles and Hungarians who, he thought, would be interested in helping him. When Chamberlain returned to Germany, to Bad Godesberg, on 22 September, Hitler said he "regretted" that the previously arranged terms were not enough. As an excuse, he alleged that the Germans of Czechoslovakia were being savagely oppressed and that the whole area should be rescued by 1 October at the latest. This meant that the Czech defenses would be occupied by the German army right away, before negotiations had even gotten under way. Chamberlain was appalled. Probably, Hitler's move was intended to push the wavering Poles and Hungarians to join him; but it looked as if Hitler wanted war, whatever the excuse. After all, if he marched into Czechoslovakia, the French and the Russians were treaty-bound to declare war, and the British of course would do so as well. Public opinion in the West was appalled: everyone at this time imagined that war would be a nightmare of smashed cities, millions upon millions of casualties, and a Bolshevik Europe at the end of it. Would Chamberlain back down? In the event, Mussolini lent a hand. In an atmosphere of panic on both sides, he proposed a four-power conference at Munich to settle the whole question. Hitler, knowing that Czechoslovakia did not split itself and that the Poles and the Hungarians would not join him in war, agreed.

The meeting, of Hitler, Ribbentrop, Chamberlain, Mussolini, Édouard Daladier, and their foreign ministers, took place in the *Führerbau* at Munich late on 29 September. Czechoslovakians waited outside to learn their fate. An agreement was signed in the early hours of the next day. Hitler was allowed to occupy the Sudetenland, and a four-power commission would establish the new boundaries. Relations between Hitler and the foreigners were tolerably good. Chamberlain told him fishing stories. Daladier swapped anecdotes about the war. Hitler was full of contempt for them both and later called them "little worms." He himself drove into the Sudetenland and said the Munich agreement of 30 September was "an undreamt-of triumph, so great that you can scarcely imagine it." He had obtained the Czech defenses without firing a shot. The Poles and Hungarians then moved to amputate other parts of Czechoslovakia. Internal change there also brought about the resignation of poor Beneš and the creation of a federal system, in which the Slovaks obtained autonomy. "Czecho-Slovakia," as it was now called, obtained a four-power guarantee. Hitler was not at all pleased that it was still there.

6

1939

MOST BRITISH PEOPLE, when asked about the origins of the Second World War, would give a simple answer: Hitler. His view of things was not the same. For him, eastern Europe was part of a German power bloc; had not the British implicitly recognized as much when they threw away their Czechoslovakian card? True, there were voices in Great Britain, notably Churchill's, that warned against concession to Germany and demanded feverish rearmament, which the Chamberlain government was alleged (wrongly) to be pursuing in dilatory fashion. But did not the British move over Munich mean that, though the British statesmen might have to cause trouble in public for the sake of their own political position at home, they would back down in the end? Far from toning down his aggressive plans and joining the club of European states, even perhaps accepting the African colonies that might be offered him, Hitler went ahead with his plans for the reshaping of eastern Europe. There were many excuses for him to act.

Of these, the first was supplied by the Slovaks. They were restive under Czechoslovakian rule, but they were worried about breaking off from that rule, because Hungary, to whom Slovakia had belonged before 1918, might attempt to take it over. Politics in Bratislava, the Slovak capital city, became extremely confused, with a somewhat divided Nationalist, anti-Semitic Party led by a priest, Josef Tiso, dictating the pace of affairs. Hitler determined to use the Slovaks as a tool for bringing about the disintegration of Czechoslovakia. German emissaries encouraged Slovak intransigence toward Prague over the kind of dreary dispute that unfailingly occurs when two nationalisms are in conflict within the same state. The Czechs attempted to use force. Hitler then instructed the Slovaks to declare their independence if they wished to avoid being handed over to Hungary. Ribbentrop drafted the declaration, which a trembling Tiso read out in Bratislava on 13 March.

With Slovakia a German satellite, what was to become of "Czechia"? By now, Prague was run by timid, conservative, and even pro-German elements, terrified of any possibility that Communists might save them from Germany. Emil Hácha, the new president, wished to save his country from further destruction and invited himself to Berlin to appeal to Hitler. He arrived in Berlin on 14 March and, in a state so agitated that he had a mild stroke, discussed matters humbly with Hitler. He agreed to sign away his country's independence. Hitler had always considered Bohemia and Moravia ("Czechia") as part of historic Germany, Czechs or no Czechs, and he wanted the Czech arms industry. He proclaimed a "Protectorate," even allowing a Czech government to remain in existence. On 15 March he entered the country, arriving in Prague early the following day. A week later, rounding off his gains, he casually issued an ultimatum to Lithuania demanding for Germany the German-inhabited port of Klaipeda (Memel).

The British then stirred. They had been unable to act to save Czecho-Slovakia, because it had, after all, broken up ostensibly from within. But a message now passed, loudly and clearly, to British public opinion: Hitler's notion of diplomacy was to send in his tanks, bully harmless old men, and institute a reign of terror in the conquered country. With every day that passed, were not submarines and bombing aircraft being built in profusion? Where would it stop? In earlier days, some British politicians had piously hoped that Hitler would invade Russia and destroy Communism. Now, all sensible ones dreaded that possibility, because a Hitler in charge of Russia's resources would, they imagined, create a vast Eurasian bloc that would rapidly extinguish Great Britain and France. Chamberlain still hoped for a miracle, but the days of appeasement had gone. Hitler had promised before that he would stop. But he had gone on and on. What next?

It turned out to be Danzig. Danzig, later Gdańsk, was a German-inhabited city at the mouth of the Vistula. It was important for Poland's trade, and the Poles had tried to annex it, together with the other lands they had taken from Germany in 1919. But the city was so adamantly German that Lloyd George had proposed for it the status of a free city, guaranteed by the League. Now, Hitler outlined to the Poles his ideas

for a German-Polish relationship. No doubt what he would have preferred would have been for Poland to act the part of Slovakia; after
all, Poland had territorial claims against Russia and could well have
acted as an ally to Germany in the event of an invasion of Russia. As a
symbol, almost, of German domination of the East, Hitler wanted Danzig to be taken back into the Reich.

Rather to his surprise, the Poles objected. They had learned the lessons of Schuschnigg, Beneš and Hácha: never make any concession at
all to Hitler. They greatly overrated their own military prowess and
behaved with all the mad bravery of their legendary Polish noble class,
the *szlachta*. The British then took a hand. They were worried that
Poland would join the German side, and so felt they had to offer Poland
something concrete. Besides, there was alarm that Germany would invade Romania, with her oil, and only the Poles were near enough to
help Romania. The British greatly overrated Polish strength. Their foreign minister, the ineffable Lord Halifax, remarked in cabinet, "There
can be no doubt that Poland is a more worthwhile ally than the Soviet
Union." They offered Poland a territorial guarantee, which the Poles
accepted on 31 March. Then they offered similar guarantees to other
small states, none of them even remotely menaced by Hitler.

Hitler determined to challenge the British, and to risk the war that
they loudly and often threatened in the event of a German attack on
Poland. This time, Hitler was warned that the West would not back
down. Feeling against him ran too high in London; he could choose the
most favorable pretext under the sun, but still the British would go to
war if he transgressed the bounds of diplomatic propriety and went
ahead with his bullying of small states.

Underneath the official British attitude of firmness, Hitler could sense
some softness and irresolution, for, after all, war for the sake of Danzig
hardly made sense. Highly placed men in the Chamberlain government
were associated with an offer to Germany of a loan of one billion British
pounds to help her "over the difficulties of disarmament." Colonies were
mentioned. Above all, the British made, apparently, no serious effort to
come to terms with the one power in the East that could do anything to
oppose Germany solidly — the Soviet Union. An approach to Stalin had
been made, in the early summer, with a view to alliance. But were the
British serious? Were they not simply "chalking a Red bogey on the wall
in the hope that Hitler would run away"? The nature of the negotiations
suggested so. The delegation went to Russia by slow boat and made
problems over small matters. In effect, the British thought that Stalin's
Russia was too disorganized after the hideous turmoil of the 1930s

ever to stand up to Hitler; in any case, they feared the consequences of a Russian victory hardly less than they feared the consequences of a German one. Their negotiations with Stalin looked, and probably were, something of a sham. Both Hitler and Stalin guessed as much.

Again, Hitler had drawn up a plan for attack on Poland, "Case White." The last alleged date on which the army could move was, this time, 26 August, ostensibly because, thereafter, the mud would be too much for the tanks. Early that month Hitler told his generals and his Italian allies (who, as he no doubt expected, passed it on to the British) that it was his unshakable desire to solve the Polish question by then. He also informed a highly placed neutral diplomat that "everything I am doing is directed against Russia. If the West is too stupid or too blind to see it, I shall be forced to come to an understanding with the Russians, strike at the West and after its defeat turn against the Soviet Union." In any case, he might well feel that, even if the British did declare war, they would not actually wage it. Whatever he expected, this time the nerves of the British and the Poles did not give. Despite the unofficial hints, no word came from London that a German attack on Poland would be condoned.

It was then that Hitler could move. Hints had been exchanged between Berlin and Moscow that a pact, at Poland's expense, would be thinkable. Stalin feared war; he also, no doubt, expected that the French front would hold out as in the First World War, attracting most of Hitler's forces. On 14 August, the hints culminated in a request from Hitler to Stalin for Ribbentrop to be received. This seemed to be the strangest reversal of all. Communism, the archenemy, then made its pact with nazism at the expense of democracy: as a Foreign Office wisecrack ran, "all the -isms are -wasms." On 23 August, Ribbentrop flew to Moscow. Very rapidly, he signed a pact with Stalin. Poland, by a secret agreement, would be divided between the two signatories, and there was a further agreement for division of eastern Europe into spheres of influence.

After this, Hitler hardly needed to worry: his tanks and aircraft could defeat Poland quickly, and then perhaps the West would come to its senses. As it was, would his pact with Stalin not deter them from their folly? Instead, the British ratified their alliance with Poland, and the Poles refused to move an inch. Hitler tried to bully the British with reference to his alleged military timetable. But by now the British were convinced that Hitler meant war in any event, and most of them were resolved to take a clear stand there and then. They regarded him much as they did General Idi Arnim decades later. Hitler was puzzled. He was

The Eastern Front

------- Western Boundary U.S.S.R. June, 1941

German Penetration ━━━━━━ December, 1941 ┉┉┉┉┉ November, 1942

ARCTIC OCEAN

N

WHITE
SEA

FINLAND

U.S.S.R.

Km 100 200 400
MILES
50 100 200 300

Leningrad

ESTONIA

BALTIC SEA

Riga

Volga

LATVIA

LITHUANIA

Moscow

⚑ LEEB

Minsk

Smolensk

Warsaw

⚑ BOCK

POLAND

⚑ RUNDSTEDT

Voronezh

Kiev

Don

Volga

Vinnitsa

Kharkov

Dniester

Dnepr

Uman

Donbass

Stalingrad

Prut

Odessa

ROMANIA

SEA OF
AZOV

Volga

CASPIAN SEA

BULGARIA

BLACK SEA

CAUCASUS MTS.

TURKEY

G.W. Ward

warned that the British meant business; Goering, Keitel, and Ribbentrop urged him to postpone "Case White." On 26 August he did so.
Then nothing happened. By the twenty-ninth, Hitler submitted pro-
posals to the British ambassador which amounted to a demand that a
Pole should come to Berlin and be bullied, though the terms that Hitler
spelled out as his wishes in the matter were, the ambassador had to
admit, surprisingly moderate. Some British began to think of compromise; but the Poles would not move. On 1 September, in response to this,
Hitler invaded Poland. The British and French declarations of war followed on 3 September. As Hitler's interpreter, Paul Schmidt noted,
"Hitler sat absolutely silent and unmoving. After an interval, he turned
to Ribbentrop, who had remained standing frozen by the window. 'What
now?' Hitler asked the Foreign Minister, with a furious glare, as if to say
that Ribbentrop had misinformed him about the probable reaction of
the British." But Hitler was a gambler for power. He stuck by his bet. If
the West wanted war in such circumstances, let them have it. He went to
the Anhalter Bahnhof, and entered the headquarters train that would
take him to the front in Pomerania.

Part III

The War Lord:
1939–1945

7

Victory in the West

THE SECOND WORLD WAR produced, in the end, one victor, the United States, one hero, Great Britain, one villain, Germany, and one martyr, Poland. Like many martyrs, Poland had done much to provoke her fate. Her foreign policy had been based on an extraordinary misapprehension of realities; her strategy was not any more sensible. She had nothing but the legendary courage of her men to field against the Nazis' tanks and guns; yet she put the bulk of her forces in the exposed western part of the country, in the hope of launching an attack on Berlin.

Hitler's conquest of Poland was therefore an easy matter. He invaded on 1 September. German bombers wrecked Polish communications; German tanks raced far ahead of their own infantry, caught the bulk of the Polish forces in a "pocket," reached Warsaw on 8 September, and surrounded it. On 28 September, the city was bombed into surrender. The Poles' ruin was completed when their western allies failed to help them, and the Soviet Union invaded the east of the country. Several hundred thousand Polish soldiers went into Soviet captivity and eighty thousand escaped over the southern border into Hungary or Romania, from where many made their way to the western front.

Hitler made a triumphal entry into Warsaw. He was not, himself, violently anti-Polish; he was an Austrian, and the Catholic Austrians traditionally regarded Poles with some favor. But he felt that Poland had forfeited his sympathy by her obstinacy over Danzig; and in any case his new partner, Stalin, wanted to see Poland disappear from the map. Many Germans agreed. Hitler waited for a time, to see if the western powers would now agree to discussions. When they did not, he set up a terror regime in Poland, the "Government-General" under his old legal crony, K. H. Frank, and detached large parts of the country to be ruled from Berlin. The Soviet Union took the eastern half of Poland. In all three sectors, the Polish intelligentsia, aristocracy, and clergy were persecuted and imprisoned or deported. In the "Government-General," sinister German police and SS squads, known as the *Einsatzgruppen,* kept what they called "order"—murdering and torturing on a scale that revolted German army officers. The revulsion did not achieve anything. Hitler believed that the only way to rule an occupied country was by showing who was master. The Poles were to be bullied; and they were also to be mentally enfeebled. Drink and pornographic literature were encouraged, and were sold cheaply. Three million Polish Jews either were pushed off to the Soviet sector or confined in cramped ghettos, in circumstances that caused the death of one-fifth of them in a few months. Senior army officers such as Blaskowitz complained of the cruelty and economic waste involved. Hitler stormed back at them for their "misplaced humanitarianism."

Similarly, he could not understand why Great Britain and France had gone to war for the sake of Poland. They had been unable, perhaps even unwilling, to do anything positive to save her in September 1939: the French had tiptoed over the Maginot Line, and tiptoed back again when they were fired upon. Otherwise, they made no aggressive moves; nor did the British. It was, apart from isolated incidents at sea, a sham war. Surely, Hitler supposed, the British had declared war merely for the sake of public opinion. Since their inability to do anything for Poland had been shown, would they not now make peace? Hitler did not want to harm the British Empire. He had offered guarantees late in August; in July 1940 he was even saying that its end would be a disaster for Germany. He did not bother to build submarines that might have done the British serious damage and had in 1940 only twenty-two capable of Atlantic action. He forbade bombing of open cities, of even any British or French land target. On 6 October he delivered a speech in the Reichstag that suggested a willingness to come to terms: no more war, if the British would recognize realities in the East. The British took little notice. They had gone to war, not over the rights and wrongs of the Polish-German dispute, but because Hitler was an evil man who offered the world nothing but endless bullying, terror, and conquest. They were not going to give in now.

Hitler's response was to offer the British a larger dose of the same medicine as before: he would use his army this time against France, and show the British that Germany was master of the continent. On 9 October he ordered his generals to prepare an offensive in the West. As ever, when Hitler had a plan, it was one with built-in alternatives, and a number of reasons behind it. He expounded these in a memorandum, the arguments of which he repeated several times in later speeches to the generals. The main one was that time worked for the western powers: they could count on America, and perhaps Russia as well; whereas Germany, in terms of tanks and aircraft and training, would never again be as strong as in 1940. An attack in the West might overthrow France; it would gain for Germany a good position in northeastern France; in any event, it would allow Germany to occupy Belgium and the Netherlands, which she had to do to protect her great war industries in the Ruhr from British bombing.

The generals were appalled. They did not feel that their army was strong enough to take on the French army, which was then thought, by qualified commentators, to be the strongest in the world. They overestimated, by fifteen hundred, the number of French tanks. They also feared the bombing of Germany — reacting, in other words, exactly like their counterparts in the West. They put off the attack again and again; they thought Hitler was mad, and several of them conspired, in their headquarters at Zossen, just outside Berlin, to overthrow Hitler before it was too late. Even Brauchitsch, the army's commander in chief, joined in this plot. However, when on 5 November Brauchitsch tried to talk Hitler out of his offensive, Hitler ranted at him, accusing him of cowardice. Time and again throughout the war, nervous generals would approach Hitler with a view to making him back down or make peace. Hitler would put on a command performance and leave the nervous generals once more full of faith and hope. He did this to Brauchitsch on 5 November and to assembled western-front generals on 23 November. He told them, correctly, "Behind me stands the German people. . . . In this fight I shall stand or fall." The generals gave up their plotting; Brauchitsch burned his notes and got on with planning the attack.

The generals' plan was an obvious one: Germany should violate Belgian and Dutch territory, as in 1914, and that way bypass the French defense system, the "Maginot Line." Hitler was prepared to leave things to his technicians at this stage and he did not usually interfere. Just the same, he felt that this plan was too obvious: would it not be better to send a force unexpectedly through the Ardennes region, a hilly and wooded area between the Maginot Line and the main Belgian defenses around Liège? Hitler was not alone. Erwin von Manstein, the chief of staff of the armies in the center of the German front, also thought this a good idea. He sent several memoranda to that effect, which the General Staff simply pigeonholed. The generals in Zossen (their headquarters near Berlin) thought the Ardennes impossible for tanks and mechanized troops — the roads were too few and narrow and the gradients too steep. Manstein's persistence was rewarded with dismissal from his important command: he was packed off to Poland, to command a corps. On his way through Berlin, he called upon Hitler to have his formal appointment confirmed, and there he mentioned his own ideas on the Ardennes. Hitler said of Manstein that he was "the only one who really understood me."

In any case, accident came to Hitler's aid, as it so often did. A German staff officer had taken the existing plan by plane, and had landed, after a pilot's error, in Belgium. He managed to destroy much of the plan, but the Belgians rescued it, and guessed the rest. Then, in mid-January, there was every reason to think up something else; and in due course, by mid-March, the Manstein plan was adopted, under the code name *Sichelschnitt* ("scythe sweep"). Army Group B (Fedor von Bock) would invade Belgium and the Netherlands and thereby persuade the western powers to send their best forces to defend these countries; Army Group A (commanded by field marshal Gerd von Rundstedt) would move as Manstein had planned, with strong armor, and cut off these forces in the Low Countries.

Before the Western offensive could be launched, the first clash between British and German forces occurred elsewhere, in Norway. On 9 April, Germany invaded Norway and Denmark. Later this counted as a war crime. The reality was more complicated. Scandinavia first became involved in the war because of Stalin, who, in November 1939, asked Finland to give him a strip of land close to Leningrad and some bases for the Red navy. When the Finns refused, he invaded. "The Winter War" followed, in which Finnish defense proved brave and astonishingly successful, although it collapsed in March. The British and French thought they could use this as a way of stopping both Germany and Russia: they could send "volunteers" to Finland, around the northern shores of Norway, and land them instead at Narvik, in Norway, from where they could cut the railway line that took ten million tons of Swedish iron ore every year to Germany. This plan, together with plans to mine Norwegian waters, was going ahead in the early spring of 1940. Hitler determined to forestall it; he sent a small force to Norway; German warships steamed toward Oslo.

This campaign was a brilliant one. Although only ten thousand men

were involved, bluff carried the day. A small German force of paratroops dropped at Oslo airport and staged a ceremonial entrance into
the capital. It surrendered, even though its fortress guns had crippled
one of the German warships, the battleship *Blücher*. Elsewhere it was
the same story. Two thousand Germans at Narvik held out successfully
against ten times their number of British troops, who landed well
enough but then were led with paralyzing cautiousness. After a fortnight, the whole of Norway was in German hands, though Narvik's
British garrison held on for a few weeks longer. In Denmark, which the
Germans had occupied for strategic reasons, there was next to no resistance. A single battalion took Copenhagen; the King's toy-town guards
fired a shot or two. Events were to show that passive resistance was
much more effective than the active variety.

Then, on 10 May came the great offensive in the West. This, like the
Scandinavian affair, has been shrouded in myth. The Germans have
been made out to be overwhelmingly strong — so strong that even the
best-led army and the most courageous soldiery could have done nothing. This was completely false. The Germans had 135 divisions, but
only 52 could count as proper army divisions, for the rest were made
up either of untrained or of overage men, with weak artillery. The Allies
had 130 divisions, almost all composed of trained men, and all with
stronger artillery. The Germans had 3,000 tanks, the French and British
slightly more. About a quarter of the French tanks were better than
anything the Germans had, and only a quarter were not as good as the
German Panzers I and II. In aircraft, the Germans had the edge: 3,250
to 2,500. This problem was worsened for the Allies partly because the
British kept many of their aircraft at home and partly because French
pilots would not fly as often in a day as German ones. That similar
blunders were made in the handling of tanks counted for far more in the
Allies' ultimate defeat than simple weakness in the field.

The French thought that tanks were too vulnerable to artillery and
therefore could not operate on their own. Their tanks were included in
infantry divisions. Hitler had seen things differently, and he had backed
the judgment of generals like Heinz Guderian, who appreciated that
aircraft could knock out the enemy guns while tanks raced ahead, a
hundred miles a day, to block the enemy's communications and prevent
him from retreating in an orderly way. Why did the Germans, and no
one else, hit upon this answer? In a way, because they had to. They
started arming later than others, and had to have quick results, which
the technology of tanks and aircraft could give them. But it was also
Hitler, with his uncanny intuition. Even in 1934, he had been backing

the Guderians against their more conservative rivals, such as Fritsch, who thought in terms of bulky, highly trained infantry divisions. The phrase "lightning-war" — in German, *Blitzkrieg* — had been used (from an Italian original) before 1939, and Hitler understood, now, that a united force of tanks, cooperating with aircraft like his Stukas that would dive down and bomb the enemy guns, would be able to achieve in a week or two what the infantry of 1914–1918 had been unable to manage.

*Sichelschnitt w*as also, from a strategic viewpoint, a good plan. It persuaded the Allies from the beginning that the main German attack was coming in the Low Countries; and they duly sent their best troops there. Between 10 and 15 May there was another series of brilliant military endeavors on the Germans' part. Army Group B (Bock) was not very strong, because seventy divisions had been allotted to Army Group A (Runstedt) and another twenty to Army Group C (Wilhelm von Leeb) on the passive, southern sector of the front. The Germans managed to pretend they were strong. Hundreds of paratroop dummies were dropped over Belgium and Holland. The great Belgian fortress of Eben Emael surrendered when seventy Germans, in rubber shoes, glided onto the roof of it and dropped grenades into its ventilator shafts. The Dutch canal lines were captured by a few hundred paratroops, who held the bridges long enough for the armor to come up and cross. The Dutch surrendered. To face this threat, the Allies sent in the best third of their troops, with most of their armor. They left another two-fifths in the Maginot Line, which thus served almost in a contrary sense: the Germans knew there would be no attack out of it, and equally that it could hardly be less thickly held. Their force was concentrated against the Meuse, in the center, and it was mobile, whereas the Allies had concentrated heavily on the wings.

The Allies held the central part of the front with only thirty-five divisions. Even then the exits from the Ardennes and the crossings of the river Meuse were guarded only by the few divisions of the French Second and Ninth armies. Their men were demoralized and overage; there had even been a strike in some units. They were no match for seventy fresh German divisions, and certainly could not handle seven Panzer divisions and *Stukas*.

The topographical problems of the Ardennes had been overcome by an astonishing feat of staff work; tanks, lorries, infantry, and artillery were pushed up and down the winding, narrow roads at night, well camouflaged and without the kind of traffic blockages that practically all other armies would have suffered. By 12 May, fifteen hundred tanks and fifty divisions were ready to act.

By surprise, this force burst on the French at their crossings on the Meuse north of Sedan, where the French had been defeated by the Prussians in 1870. Stukas forced the French gunners to abandon their weapons; German troops came across in all kinds of craft, even rubber dinghies, and put up pontoons for the tanks. A bridgehead was established, and then the Panzer divisions began to race southwest and west. By the next day, they were simply in a space devoid of all enemy troops. They had no problems with petrol, for they could requisition what they wanted from the garages or the French supply dumps. When they did encounter French troops, they met with little opposition, for the French, as Guderian had foreseen, were too demoralized to resist. One Panzer divisional leader, Rommel, calmly walked up to a column of French lorries, laden with troops, and ordered them to surrender. They were impressed by the sight of a German general in full uniform, and immediately did so. Spearheads reached the sea on 20 May and cut off the Allied forces in Belgium. But in any case, the Allies had been doing badly. Now they fell back, step by step, toward the Belgian coast and the coastal town of Dunkirk.

The French High Command was at a loss. It had no reserves. Maurice Gamelin, the commander, was replaced by Maxime Weygand, who ordered attacks from south and north against the German penetration. But the troops on the southern side were disorganized and those on the northern side had their hands full. Apart from a minor embarrassment with a British tank attack, on 21 and 22 May, the Germans were able to bring up their infantry and concentrate it, partly against the French to the south and partly against the British to the north. It looked as if, in the last week of May, the entire British Expeditionary Force and two French armies would be cut off in Belgium.

This did not happen. On the contrary, there occurred "the miracle of Dunkirk," in which 350,000 British and French soldiers were successfully evacuated to England by sea. Later, some suggested that Hitler had wished to spare the British any humiliation and he had therefore stopped his tanks, on 24 May, for two days, when they could have gone on to capture Dunkirk and thereby stop the British from getting away. There is no substance to this suggestion. Hitler did halt his tanks on 24 May, but he did so for sound military reasons. He knew that Ewald von Kleist, in charge of the armored divisions, had lost almost half of his tanks simply from breakdowns. He overrated the danger from the French to the south and thought that Flanders was unsuitable for tanks, because he himself had seen the terrain in the First World War. Besides, Goering was pestering him, telling him that the *Luftwaffe* would bomb the British into submission, whereas, if the tanks went in, they might be bombed by mistake. Some generals agreed with Hitler, though others did not. For two days there was a wrangle; and by the time Hitler let the tanks move again, they were too late. The Royal Air Force flew in from England to protect the Dunkirk "pocket," and by 4 June evacuation was complete.

The Allies had lost nearly half of their forces and a vast amount of ammunition. The Germans had lost only twenty-five thousand men — hardly a day's "normal wastage" in the earlier war. Weygand now tried to build up some kind of front along the Seine, but he was rapidly overwhelmed there by properly supplied German tanks. On 5 June they attacked near Rouen and northeast of Paris. They broke through the French line again. On 10 June Mussolini decided that he ought to be in on the kill and attacked France in the south. On 14 June Paris was occupied. There followed a prolonged dispute within the French government: should France fight on from her overseas empire or should she give in? The poor French had already been bled white in 1914–1918, and had gotten very little from it except moral lessons from the British and Americans about the need to forgive and forget. Few Frenchmen now had the heart to fight on; in any case, how could the British fight on, having lost their armor and most of their equipment in Belgium? A relatively new junior officer, Charles de Gaulle, led a few right-wing, nationalist followers to London. The rest of the government and the army decided for surrender. The aged Marshal Pétain, hero of the First World War, became head of state, an armistice was duly concluded on 22 June.

Adolf Hitler was in a state of ecstasy. He alone had foreseen the possible great results of a western offensive. As Alfred Jodl, chief of staff in the High Command of the armed forces, put it, "Once more Hitler's will triumphed, and his faith proved victorious. The soldiers were confronted with a miracle." The strongest army in the world had collapsed, at trivial cost to the Germans. Hitler mounted his own ceremony. The railway carriage in which German representatives had been humiliated in 1918 was taken from its museum and placed in the forest compound where it had stood in 1918. Hitler sat in Foch's chair; the German national anthem and the Party's Horst-Wessel song were played; the French monument depicting a fallen German eagle was razed; and afterward Hitler was photographed, arrogantly standing hand on hip, surveying the scene as conqueror of the West. His army occupied the north and west of France; the collaborationist Pétain regime held the south and center, and practiced unlovely right-wing politics. Hitler himself visited occupied Paris, arriving at dawn and leaving after a few hours. "The New Order" had arrived.

8

West, South, and East

HITLER HAD NOT PLANNED to be master of the West. In January 1941 he remarked, "If anyone had told me two years ago that my armies would be standing from Norway to Spain, I'd have declared him insane." But, by the end of June 1940, he was in a quandary. He had not wanted this war with the West. He let the British know, and reinforced this with a public speech, that he would make peace on what were, for him, generous terms. The British then were led, not by the vacillating Chamberlain, but by the stouthearted Churchill. The British cabinet hesitated for a time—for a longer time, in fact, than was known for many years—but decided in the end to go on with the war.

To Hitler, this was incomprehensible. Why should the British use up the last of their imperial energies in fighting a power that did not really threaten them? At a conference on 13 July he remarked that only the United States and Japan would profit from the end of the British Empire; later, when the Japanese captured Singapore, he was in a black mood. For Hitler, as for many Europeans, English ways set the tone for manners, as French ways had done in the eighteenth century. Besides, for many Europeans, England was a power myth, just as, in reverse, Prussia was for many Englishmen, and particularly, Scotsmen.

It was not as if the British could do any damage to Germany. Their blockade was ineffectual, given Germany's pact with Russia and her control of the continent. Their bomber force was too small and too far away. On the other hand, Germany could not do great harm to the British. At that time, and to some extent later, Great Britain was represented, by British propaganda, as a kind of David standing up to the German Goliath. But the English Channel was an excellent antitank ditch, the Germans had few ships, and the *Luftwaffe* — again, despite legends — was really too small to effect very much on its own. Why, then, did the British not come to terms? Why did they persist in fighting Germany, throwing away their vast resources and ending up in partnership with Stalin? There was something to be said for Hitler's point of view in this matter, and a few Englishmen said it. More have said it since. As perspective lengthens, the British war effort may, perhaps, seem to take on the character of a Hollywood epic, in which theatrical attitudes were struck while Americans put up the money and Russians supplied the extras to be shot at; after all, the bulk of the British war effort went into fighting Italians in North Africa or killing half a million German women and children by aerial bombing. But this is to misunderstand the situation of 1940. The British then saw themselves alone, against an all-powerful, monstrous empire. Narrow-minded political calculation went to the winds; Laborite, Liberal, and Tory united in detestation of Hitler's national and international immorality, and Churchill was never so popular in Great Britain as when he appeared to offer least hope and spurned Hitler's peace offer.

Certainly, in the summer of 1940, there was little consolation to offer. Hitler undertook preparations for invasion of the British Islands — "Operation Sea-lion" — in which German generals solemnly debated where they would place their troops on the English coast. They decided, rightly, that invasion would be hopeless unless the British air force was put out of action. Goering was ordered to accomplish this. August and the first half of September marked the "Battle of Britain," in which Goering's efforts to knock out the RAF fighters failed.

British propaganda brilliantly suggested that the country was fighting heroically against heavy odds. Churchill was more realistic when, at the height of the invasion scare, with the German army only twenty miles over the Channel, he sent the bulk of the remaining armor to North Africa. It was true that the Germans had twenty-five hundred aircraft to the RAF's thousand; it was also true that the British had a temporary weakness in their very limited numbers of trained pilots. On the other hand, they had radar stations which gave good warning when the Germans came; their aircraft could climb in time to fight off German aircraft which suffered from limited fuel; and in any case most of the British planes were fighters, which were faster and far less vulnerable than the bombers that made up two-thirds of the German aircraft strength. German tactics were also based on inexperience, so that the

Luftwaffe's superior numbers did not play as great a part as they might. Serious harm might have been dealt to the RAF had the airfields and radar stations been systematically attacked. This happened only for a few days, from 24 August to 5 September, after which the *Luftwaffe*'s energies were concentrated on the bombing of London. By mid-September, the British had won, knocking out 1,735 German aircraft for a loss of 915. Since, by 1940 (and even 1939), the British were producing 600 aircraft per month to the Germans' 450, Goering could not go on.

The planned, day-time, campaign was given up. Instead, from 6 September, German energies went into the night bombing of London: the "Blitz," as it was inaccurately called. The city of London and, later, other British cities were regularly bombed, and sixty thousand casualties were incurred. The Londoners, especially, could be rightly proud of their courage and endurance in an experience that the authorities, before 1939, had thought would cause a demand for one million places in lunatic asylums. Everyone had expected the "Blitz" from Hitler and had even been surprised when it did not happen in September 1939. This too was a myth. Hitler did not want to bomb open cities. He had bombed Warsaw, but that had been a defended military target. He had bombed Rotterdam, but that had happened only because the *Luftwaffe* commander had not been told in time that the Dutch had sued for an armistice, and again because it counted as a defended military target. Hitler did not mean to bomb London. He did so because of an accident, brought about by the British blackout. A German flyer jettisoned his bomb load over what he took to be empty countryside. It turned out to be London. The British then sent bombers on a raid over Berlin; and this caused Hitler to promise revenge on London. The "Blitz" went on regularly until the spring of 1941, when British air power grew too strong and the *Luftwaffe* was needed elsewhere.

There was not much that Hitler could do. There were only some twenty oceangoing German submarines and when the British were given fifty old American destroyers their convoys could be well protected. There were too few German capital ships to do much damage to British trade: *Scharnhorst* and *Gneisenau* were penned in; when *Bismarck* came out, in May 1941, she was sunk. It would be some time before Germany could produce the bombers and U-boats that alone could attack Great Britain directly.

However, Hitler could attack her in the Mediterranean. His Italian allies had advanced into British-held Egypt and his closest generals, Keitel and Jodl, favored helping them. How? The Italians said they did not want direct help in the desert. The only way was, therefore, through Spain: Gibraltar, a British colony at the gates of the Mediterranean, might be seized from Spain, and perhaps a great Franco-Spanish bloc could be built up to help Germany there. Hitler saw Mussolini on the Brenner Pass on 4 October and then went to see the Spanish leader, Francisco Franco, at Hendaya on 23 October. That meeting was not a success. Franco annoyed Hitler with his peculiarly Latin combination of pride, obstinacy, and parasitism. He doubted if the British were defeated; he had been warned off by the Americans; his country was starving, after its devastating civil war. Besides, he was in close touch with an old friend in Berlin, Admiral Canaris, head of German military intelligence, who told him not to help Hitler, whom Canaris opposed. Hitler steamed away again, furious that he had helped the "reactionaries and moneybags" around Franco. He then met the aged Pétain at Montoire. Pétain would help only if he could send troops to Morocco, an idea that Hitler disliked. Otherwise, not much could be done.

It was Mussolini who found an answer to this impasse; but it was not one to Hitler's liking. Mussolini attacked Greece as part of his own drive to create an Italian empire in the Mediterranean. The invasion was not a success. By the end of October, the Italians had been stopped in the Epirus and had been driven back in an epic of vainglory and muddle. By December, their foreign minister had to admit that, "ridiculous and grotesque" as it might seem, they might have to ask for an armistice. Hitler was worried about all of this—not because of the Greeks, toward whom he had no ill will, but because the British could use Greek bases to invade the Balkans. In particular, they could send bombers into Romania's oil fields. These, located mainly in the Ploieşti area, supplied Germany with seven of the ten million tons she needed annually. To obviate this problem, he offered to mediate between Italy and Greece. The Greeks would have none of this: they were proud of their effort. So Hitler had to think in terms of direct help for the Italians. In this way, his generals planned an invasion of Greece, "Operation Marita."

Hitler had been brought into the Balkans for other reasons as well, which had little to do with Mussolini, but a great deal to do with his Russian deal. The pact had guaranteed to Stalin a share of Poland and the right to occupy former Tsarist-Russian territories in eastern Europe. Stalin profited from this in June 1940. As France fell, the Red army occupied the three Baltic Republics and later moved into the northeastern province of Romania, Bessarabia. Would Stalin threaten Hitler's oil?

The alarm was immediate and Hitler began to build up his bloc. He secretly sent weapons to the Finns, who feared fresh Russian demands. In August, he decided to clear up, once and for all, the Hungaro-Romanian border dispute that had been disturbing central European peace for two decades: the disputed province of Transylvania was divided between the two countries with as little unfairness as could be managed. Bulgaria was also bribed with a part of the Romanian Black Sea coast. The king of Romania abdicated and was replaced by his young son, Michael, with Marshal Antonescu as effective head of an anti-Semitic, semi-Fascist state. Antonescu wanted German protection; he accepted a German military mission in October. It proved to be the nucleus of a powerful German force.

Hitler was glad to have Antonescu's alliance, for the Romanian was a man after his own heart: authoritarian, anti-Semitic, unaffected by sentiment, and extremely anti-Soviet. Hitler said of him that he was the only one of his allied statesmen to have "vision." German blandishment of the Bulgarians followed, for they would have to let German troops through their country to attack Greece. Gradually, the Balkan countries, competing with each other for Hitler's favor, accepted alliance with him. Germany, Italy, and Japan had formed the "Tripartite Pact" on 27 September, providing for mutual assistance in their various regions of expansion. Then, in November, Romania, Hungary, and Slovakia joined; in March, Bulgaria and Yugoslavia (Yugoslavia very briefly indeed).

This new bloc was really intended as a counter to Russia. Stalin had irritated Hitler with his interference in the south and in the Baltic. At times the Russians would behave in a less unfriendly spirit towards the British ambassador and such thaws alarmed Hitler who, from time to time, responded by declaring that his real interest was war with Russia — his "life's mission," as he said after one such alarm at the end of July. Then Russian behavior, with regard to Germany, would improve, and the alarm would pass. There was an amicable enough exchange of territory between the two powers; German colonies that had lived in Russia since the eighteenth century were peacefully repatriated; Stalin went on delivering the goods that Germany needed, in great quantities and at reasonable prices.

There were, therefore, two strands at least in Hitler's thinking about Stalin. On the one hand, he sometimes reflected that what he had always really wanted was an empire at Russia's expense; on the other, he saw that he already had a war with the West on his hands and perhaps could use the East to help him win it. Throughout the last half of 1940, first one, then the other, strand was uppermost. By November, however, it was clear that Stalin entertained menacing ambitions. To clear up the difficulties, Stalin sent his foreign minister, Vyacheslav Molotov, to Berlin in mid-November. Molotov trotted stonily through his paces, in the manner that was to irritate statesmen of all countries for the next decade. Hitler was duly irritated. He offered Molotov a tempting prospect: join the Tripartite Pact, and Russia could have the straits of Constantinople and southern central Asia, including Persia. Molotov was unmoved by this grand prospect. He looked at the fine print. German attempts to overcome his pawnbroker haggling were not helped when a British bombing raid forced the party into an air raid shelter. Molotov could well say, "If the British have been defeated, then what are we doing in this cellar?" He wanted concrete concessions at once, and a Soviet note later set them out: no German troops in Finland; Soviet bases in the Baltic as far west as Denmark; a Soviet presence in Bulgaria; objections to the German presence in Romania. There was, in other words, no common ground. Hitler lost patience and decided that in 1941 he would attack Russia. He did not answer Molotov's note. Instead, in Directive number 21 of 18 December, his generals were ordered to prepare plans for an invasion of Russia — "Operation Barbarossa."

Hitler later offered all kinds of reasons for this. At times, he made out that conquest of Russia was his life's work. At other times, he said that a Russian move forward would be "the end of *Mitteleuropa*—the Balkans and Finland are endangered flanks." Sometimes he pretended, quite absurdly, that Stalin had been dishonest in his economic dealings; sometimes he said that Russia was arming so fast that she must have aggression in mind. Generally, however, Hitler offered more plausible reasoning. If the British were still fighting, he would say, it must be because they had a secret deal with Stalin. If Germany waited until 1942, when the Americans were strong enough to intervene, it would be too late. Russia was Great Britain's sword in Europe and the British would never make peace until Russia had been knocked out.

The background to all of this was Hitler's supposition that Nazi Germany was much stronger than Soviet Russia. This was an extraordinary misjudgment; indeed, in retrospect it was Hitler's greatest mistake. But it was one that, at the time, almost everyone endorsed. Not many people believed in the efficacy of socialism, let alone communism, as opposed to the kind of economic virility that fascism was supposed to represent. Stalin's Russia was, from the point of view of the propagandist, her own worst enemy: she had starvation, inefficiency, and tyranny on an appalling scale. The German generals expected that they would overthrow

Russia in six weeks or so. Hitler himself said, "we'll kick the door in and the house will fall down." The military planners went ahead in an astonishingly slapdash way, obviously expecting that Russia would fall apart into conflicting classes and races at the first appearance of a Panzer. On the whole, outsiders agreed with this. British Intelligence estimated Russia's likely survival at about six weeks. American Intelligence was rather more generous and thought three months. Did Stalin himself imagine that he would survive for even a fortnight? His policy makes little sense except on such a supposition. He ignored everyone's warnings, and he ignored, too, the obvious buildup of German troops on his western borders. He went on presenting the Germans with great quantities of grain, oil, and precious metals such as manganese or tungsten — enough, indeed, to keep the German invasion going for 1941. The German attack on Russia seemed, at the time, the least foolhardy enterprise that Hitler had ever launched.

Things would not be manageable until the spring, and in the meantime Hitler had to make sure that there would be no trouble to his rear. He authorized the generals to go ahead with "Marita" against Greece. In March, the German Twelfth Army in Romania received permission to enter Bulgaria. Again there was an astonishing feat of staff work, in which even barracks were sent out from Germany to house the otherwise exposed soldiers. The plan even survived what might otherwise have been an appalling shock; for, later in the month, the Germans found themselves with a Yugoslavian problem.

Yugoslavia, under her regent, Prince Paul, had had to engage in a humiliating competition for Hitler's favor with Bulgaria, Hungary, and Italy. Prince Paul disliked Nazi Germany, but could see no other course. He adhered to the Tripartite Pact on 25 March. Then the British exploded their political bomb: they had encouraged dissident Serbian nationalists to overthrow Prince Paul and they had promised support. The Yugoslavian coup occurred on 27 March. Hitler's flank was deeply threatened, and he again managed an astonishing piece of military strategy in getting the Second Army to Austria in time. Troops were marched through Hungary (the prime minister of which, Count Teleky, committed suicide in shame at his country's dishonor) and on 6 April they invaded. Belgrade was bombed for three days as "punishment." At the same time, the Twelfth Army went on into Greece. Neither the Yugoslavian nor the Greek army could stand up to Stukas and tanks any more than the French. Within ten days, Yugoslavian resistance was at an end, and by 23 April, so was the Greek — the Greek prime minister also committing suicide. Yugoslavia was divided into zones and Croatia became independent under a pro-German Fascist government, led by the horrible Ante Pavelić. Greece was simply occupied.

This whole campaign ended in another brilliant stroke by the Germans. The British had indeed sent help to the Greeks, and to do so they had interrupted their victories against Italy in North Africa. Now, Hitler sent a small tank force to Africa, Rommel's *Afrika-Korps*, which won amazing victories in a few days in April — victories won with Volkswagens that had been dressed up to look, from the air, like tanks, and that continued because Rommel captured so many British supplies. In May, the British forces sent to help Greece also suffered defeat. They had been evacuated to Crete, which Churchill wished to keep as an air base. By surprise attack, German paratroops, four thousand strong, captured the island from a British force ten times their number. On 1 June the British evacuated the island, in chaos. The facts of the situation did not prevent them from claiming that they had lost only to overwhelming German might. Europe was then clear: Hitler could begin his greatest battle.

9

Barbarossa: 1941

"WE'LL BE INVINCIBLE. When we fight, Europe will hold its breath," said Hitler before "Barbarossa." The whole world had every reason to hold its breath, as three million Germans and their allies struck against Stalin at dawn on Sunday, 22 June. Every participant in that campaign remembered its first days as a kind of crusade. "For the German soldier," a communiqué had stated in mid-June, "nothing is impossible." This also was Stalin's opinion. Right up to the last moment, he continued to "appease" Hitler in ways that were calamitous for the Red army.

He did not react to the buildup of a huge German force in Poland and accepted German explanations that it had to do with a vast camouflage operation designed to disguise a new plan to invade England. He sent back German pilots who crash-landed in Russia while surveying the west of the country with cameras. He regarded any warning of Hitler's intentions as "provocation," and even had a German deserter shot when he came over and told the Russians that they were about to be attacked. When the German invasion came, Stalin retired, in a state of catalepsy, for ten days and did not speak on the radio until 3 July; when Molotov received German Ambassador Schulenburg and his declaration of war, he gaped: "What have we done to deserve this?"

Stalin had every reason for his panic. The Red army was caught, through his fault, in the middle of a complicated reorganization. In the years 1937–1939 Stalin had had almost all of the senior officers and three-quarters of the middle-ranking ones shot or taken to labor camps. The army was then mainly run by the kind of granite-brained brute who surfaces in the later stages of most dictatorships — toadies from below, sadists from above, whose only military tactic was futile, suicidal attack: Budyonny, Mekhlis, and Shchadenko. Naturally enough, they had little understanding of modern techniques. The Red army had been quite innovative in the 1920s and the early 1930s, many of its designers being men of deserved reputation abroad. Its new tanks, the T-34 and KV series, were very good, for they could both knock out the standard German tanks of that period and resist German antitank gunnery. But the tanks had been held up because Kulik, who headed the Red artillery, thought, "The artillery will shoot all your tanks to pieces. Why produce them?" There was no radar. Mines were dismissed as a cowardly device. Klimenty Voroshilov thought that tank divisions were "a very farfetched idea." The outstanding aircraft designer, Tupolev, had been put into a labor camp in 1938. Pilots had had only fifteen hours of training in their new machines; lorry drivers had had an hour's practice; and 44 percent of the tanks needed refitting. The Red army was of course large enough, having as many men as the Germans and their allies. It had 12,000 aircraft and 10,000 tanks, although fewer than 2,000 of them were modern ones of the T-34 or KV classes. The Germans had 3,350 aircraft, all of better design than most of the Russian ones, and 3,550 tanks, not equal to the T-34's but better than the other Russian ones. There was no reason, in terms of material alone, for the Germans to do so well. But there was every reason in terms of leadership.

There was also a great imponderable. How had Stalin's behavior affected the morale of the ordinary Soviet soldier, whether Russian, Ukrainian, Georgian, Cossack, or collectivized *muzhik*? Would they fight for Stalin or would they give in at once? One Russian commander telegraphed back to Moscow, in the first days of the war, "Soviet troops are fighting," as if it were a matter for surprise. Stalin's own strategy really made sense only if he supposed that if the Red army were allowed to maneuver, it would fall apart. Hitler himself guessed as much, though he had not much more time for the non-Russian nationalities of the Soviet state than he had for the Russians themselves. In March, he ordered the army to shoot all Communist commissars, for once they were out of the way, Russia would fall apart: "the ideological bond is not yet strong enough to hold them together."

Much of Stalin's weakness had registered with Hitler, and this accounts for the slapdash way in which he and the German High Command behaved. They wanted to prosecute the war against Great Britain, and therefore decreased production for the army on an average, between July and December 1941, by 38 percent, so as to have more resources to spare for the navy and air force. In July 1940, thirty-five infantry divisions had been disbanded. Certainly, the number of Panzer divisions was doubled, from the original ten, but this was achieved by halving the number of tanks in each one, to 160. No preparations at all were made for a Russian winter campaign, with fatal results when the winter duly came. On 22 June 1941, there was ammunition for only "one month's major combat expenditure" and fewer resources, generally, than there had been for the western campaign in 1940.

The Red army fielded 118 infantry, 20 cavalry, and 40 motorized divisions while the Germans put up 118 infantry (of which the Finns gave 16 and the Romanians 15), 15½ motorized, and 19 Panzer divisions. However, whereas the Red army could call on plentiful reserves, at least another 125 divisions, the Germans could only just cover losses with fresh conscripts and had too few new aircraft and tanks. Clearly, they had to win outright victory straight away, in a great frontier battle. Because of this, they were very unclear as to their real objectives. Some of the planners thought in terms of Leningrad and Kiev; others wanted to make for Moscow; in "war games" staged at Zossen there was prattling about "the general line from Archangel to Astrakhan."

Something of a compromise resulted. There were three army groups — North (Leeb), Center (Bock), and South (Rundstedt). Center, with 930 tanks and 50 divisions, was not really strong enough to fight a frontier battle on its own and then plunge forward to Moscow; on the other hand, neither North, with 570 tanks, nor South, with 750, were strong enough to undertake capture of such far-flung objectives as Leningrad and Kiev. Especially in Bock's group, there would be a tremendous tussle between the tank commanders, such as Guderian, who wanted to reach out far ahead of the infantry, and infantry commanders like Kluge, commander of the Fourth Army, who would wish the tanks to stay behind and help him clear up the great masses of Russian soldiery who had been cut off by the initial tank drive. This problem would become immensely complicated by problems of climate and terrain. In France, the tanks had had only 250 miles to travel in order to reach the Channel. Then they had had to stop for a lengthy refitting. With aircraft, it had been much the same: between March and June 1940, the *Luftwaffe* had lost 2,784 aircraft over a limited airspace. In Russian circumstances, the tanks would be strained by the muddy, dusty terrain, the paucity of roads, and the nonexistence of civilian fuel supply; and the aircraft would have to cover an area much vaster than France. A campaign similar in scale to the French one would merely carry the Germans as far as Smolensk, on the upper Dniepr, and that was still four hundred miles from Moscow. These problems came up, though in a haphazard way, even in German plans.

To start with, however, Russian blundering allowed the Germans to pretend that these problems did not matter. On 22 June itself, far too much of the Red army had been stationed just on the frontier. It had given up the "Stalin Line," which had been prepared along the prewar frontier, but it had not yet prepared a proper line along the new border. Too much of the army had been crammed into "salients" that jutted out into German-held territory and were, therefore, vulnerable to attack from three sides and to bombing. Besides, the bulk of the Red air force in the frontier areas was knocked out at once. German bombers flew high, to escape radar detection (not that any existed), and then dove, steeply and invisibly out of the rising sun. Twenty-five hundred Red aircraft were knocked out in two days, the bulk of them on the ground. Then the Germans assaulted the salients. In the one at Bialystok, three divisions shot their commissars and surrendered. Another six were cut off, together with twenty-five hundred tanks (almost all of those available in the central area) which were too tightly packed to deploy even if their drivers had known how to do so.

Guderian's tanks on the southern wing and Hoth's on the northern one raced through gaps, followed by their infantry in motor vehicles, and passing messages by radio to their escorting Stukas. Within five days, the "pincers" closed at Slonim, a hundred miles to the east. Fifteen Russian divisions were caught, west of them, in the Minsk pocket. Three hundred thousand men fell prisoner a few days later. The Russians had another disaster on the northern front. Quite soon, it had lost contact with the central one, and Hoepner's tanks probed the open flank, pushing the Russians back again and again and capturing the various river bridges by clever ruses. Not even the KV-Is and KV-IIs that the Red army used here were any help to it. These fifty-two-ton tanks, with eighty-millimeter armor plating, were so tough that German shells could do them no damage. They could be knocked out only if a German tank maneuvered to very close range from the side and fired horizontally. Russian tactics were so primitive and cooperation among infantry, aircraft, and tanks so poor that the lighter German tanks were able to maneuver with great agility, using their radios, to defeat the monster tanks. By early July, Army Group North stood at Riga, menacing Leningrad, though Army Group South had a harder job in southern Poland, not least because the Russian commander, Kirponos, did not lose his nerve as his counterpart Kuznetsov had done in the Baltic.

Still, there were problems in the center. Guderian and Hoth, with their armor, wished to go racing far ahead; but the infantry commanders, on the whole, demanded their help in reducing the Russian "pockets," for many Russians threatened to escape from them because the German cordon was so thin; besides — unlike the case in France — Russian soldiers proved to be very tough, and they fought on, even though surrounded. Hitler was called in to mediate in this dispute. He took the prudent view advanced by the army's High Command and the infantry generals, and he was much criticized for this after the war. This criticism was unrealistic. Western Russia, with so few roads and, on occasion, such appalling mud, was not ideal either for tanks or for rapid infantry follow-up. A Panzer advance was "a strange spectacle from the air — stationary Panzer blobs strung out across the landscape for a distance of a hundred miles or more" whenever it rained. Hitler preferred not to let Guderian go too far ahead. By 9 July, he had reached and crossed the upper Dniepr near Smolensk. By mid-month, Army Group Center's infantry had managed to seal off most of the Russians caught west of this river; another three hundred thousand went into captivity. Guderian grumbled that if he had gone on toward Moscow at this stage, the war might have been ended at a stroke.

Yet Hitler in his new headquarters in East Prussia, near the small town of Rastenburg, had always to take the overall view; and, as he reassured another general later on, he was sure that "things become clearer at a distance." In mid-July, both of the other two army groups were some way behind the flanks of Center and both were appealing for more help in the form of tanks. Besides, the gaps on Center's flanks were now threatened by counterattacks — indeed, the first serious Russian success in the war occurred toward the end of July, in an attack at Yelnya and Gomel, between Smolensk and Kiev, where Center's flank came under pressure. Center's victories were therefore illusory, and Guderian's course would only mean empty advances. Besides, it had all been costly: 200,000 casualties by mid-July, and 1,284 tanks lost by Center alone, which now possessed only 960. The troops began to tire, once they were cheated of the frontier victory they had thought would end the whole campaign. As General Hasso von Mauteuffel has described it, "The spaces seemed endless, the horizon nebulous. We were depressed by the monotony of the landscape and the immensity of the stretches of forest, marsh and plain. Good roads were so few and rain quickly turned the sand or loam into a morass. The villages looked wretched and melancholy with their straw-thatched wooden houses. Nature was hard, and the human beings were just as hard and insensitive, indifferent to weather, hunger and thirst, and almost as indifferent to life and losses, pestilence and famine. The Russian civilian was tough and the Russian soldier tougher still."

The dispute over the use of tanks then became complicated by a further one over objectives. In the last ten days of July, Brauchitsch and Halder tried to convince Hitler that he should make for Moscow, and Bock supported them. Moscow had great symbolical importance and it was also the center of Russia's best railway network, which could dispatch troops faster than the Germans could over land. Hitler thought Moscow did not matter so much. Perhaps he had one of his intuitions that the war would last beyond the winter; in any event, he said that the proper objectives then should be, on the one hand, Leningrad, "the poisonous nest from which Asiatic venom is spewed into the Baltic," the fall of which would put heart into the Finns, and, on the other hand, the great plains of southern Russia, with their mineral wealth, and the Crimea, which could act "as a gigantic aircraft carrier" from which the Russians could strike at Romanian oil. Besides, both Army Groups North and South were in need of help. They demanded tanks from Center, claiming that otherwise they could not effect any serious successes.

At this stage, Hitler still listened to his technicians. They, after all, had carried out the rearmament and the training that had had such outstanding results in 1939 and 1940. The Army Commander Brauchitsch was a large and imposing figure; his chief of staff, Halder, wore an air of professorial dyspepsia and intense competence. General von Bock was every inch the Junker general. Hitler had supported the technicians before. But the experience of Barbarossa convinced him that he alone had the real answers. He ordered Guderian, on Bock's right flank, and Hoth, on his left flank, to assist Army Groups South and North. Halder was appalled at Hitler's juggling with Panzer corps as if they were mere pins on a map, and he urged Guderian simply to ignore Hitler's orders and plow on: "a radical improvement is not to be expected unless operations become so fluent that his tactical thinking is overtaken by events." Hitler flew to Bock's headquarters at Smolensk on 30 July. There, not for the last time, he was overruled by the giant Bock. The result was a compromise: Guderian should stay with Center for two weeks, refit, and then move south. This happened. Guderian broke through the Russian lines at Roslavl, broke up their grouping near Gomel, and then refitted. As Hitler had imagined, his actions did help the left wing of Army Group South to win a substantial victory at Uman, northwest of Kiev, early in August. Guderian still wanted to move on Moscow, and flew to Rastenburg on 20 August to see his

Führer. There, he found an atmosphere of high tension. As soon as he arrived, Brauchitsch told him, "I forbid you to mention Moscow." Halder had gone to bed, in a state of nervous exhaustion.

Yet Hitler's intuition was probably correct. The Russians standing before Bock had now begun to understand how a defense against pincer movements should be waged. Bock's group was running short of everything. There were important prizes to be won elsewhere; and Bock's tank groups could help gain them. On 25 August, after refitting, both Hoth and Guderian turned their tanks away from Center. On Hoth's side, the effect on the Russians defending the Baltic area was electric. Their flanks were turned, and by early September the Germans had advanced to within a few miles of Leningrad, capturing a large Russian force on Lake Ilmen, and cutting the railway line from Leningrad to Moscow at Tikhvin, where they established a salient. Leningrad was now surrounded, and Hitler proposed to have it starved and then razed to the ground. His forces here met up with the Finns, just over the waters of Lake Ladoga.

On the southern side, there was an immense victory. Guderian moved south, toward the eastern approaches to Kiev, at the very moment Timoshenko was organizing a huge Russian counterattack west of the city. The German infantry stopped Timoshenko's attack, which was conducted in the usual bungling style, while Kleist's armor came up from the southwest and Guderian's from the northeast. Between 16 and 20 September, Timoshenko's huge force was caught in a pocket at Kiev, the Germans taking 665,000 prisoners. Nothing much opposed Army Group South as it went on into the Ukraine. Odessa fell on 16 October; Kharkov on 24 October; the Donbass, the center of Russian coal mining and hydroelectricity, in November. It was only after he had captured Rostov-on-the-Don, gateway to the Caucasus, that Rundstedt's drive petered out in midmonth. The resulting industrial and mineral booty was such that Germany was able to fight on until 1942. All of this was an obvious vindication of Hitler's strategy. An attack on Moscow, even if successful, would merely have secured a great deal of marsh and steppe.

However, in late September, after Center had been virtually passive for two months, the action returned to the Moscow theater. Halder and Bock could now plan their sweep forward to Moscow: "Operation Typhoon." Eighty divisions were assembled, with two thousand tanks, since Hoth, Hoepner, and Guderian had been diverted back to Center. Russian strength was, then, rather poor in tanks, even obsolete ones, and Russian air strength was pitiful, because the factories had not started to produce again after their shift to the East. They had only numerical strength. When Hitler issued his order for "Typhoon," he exulted: "I say this today because for the first time I am entitled to say it. The enemy is already broken, and will never rise again." Ribbentrop emanated an obscene confidence. Hitler lost himself in speculations as to the shape of his new empire in the East: there would be vast *Autobahnen*, stretching from Trondheim in Norway to the Crimea, which he would turn into a German Riviera. Isolated colonies of German soldier-farmers would lord it in garrisons over a grunting Slavonic populace. There would be an enormous wall along the Urals, by which the German possessions would be protected from the antics of the remaining Russians in Siberia. As to them, they might as well remain Bolshevik — "It will be our guarantee of their permanent ignorance." Indeed, Stalin could even be left in charge: he was after all a great man, and had accomplished a near miracle in what he had managed to do with this "Slav rabbit-family." As to the Slavs on the German side of the wall, they need only be taught to sign their names, count up to twenty-five, and read the traffic signs, to avoid being run over. "The Volga will be our Mississippi," said Hitler. The last act of conquest was now due.

Guderian, from the south, led off on 30 September, and the other groups to the north began on 2 October. There was instant success. Guderian broke through the Russian flank, took Oryol to block a Russian retreat, and struck forward to Tula, which the Germans invaded while its trams were still running. By 4 October, on this southern side, a large Russian pocket was formed around the city of Bryansk, on the Desna. On the other side, similar, but less spectacular, maneuvering brought another large pocket by 7 October at Vyazma, both towns being roughly halfway between Smolensk and Moscow. There was, again, contention over tanks, but this time Russian resistance inside the two pockets was such that the dispute did not go far: the tanks were needed too much by the infantry. Vyazma fought on until 13 October, Bryansk until 21 October. Another six hundred thousand men were taken prisoner. In Moscow, there was panic. The government streamed out in automobiles; there was looting; Lenin's body was removed from its mausoleum on Red Square; whores invaded the Savoy Hotel; the Moscovites bought up German dictionaries; the *Luftwaffe* bombed them. Hitler was in a state of jubilation. When the Bryansk pocket was sealed, he could not eat a thing and sat paralyzed in self-satisfaction, even though, that day, Himmler arrived to celebrate his birthday. Everyone thought Russia would then collapse. Bock gathered his strength for the final effort to take Moscow. In the latter two weeks of October, his men fought their way forward, in places, to within forty miles of the city.

The final offensive began on 15 November and went on for just over a fortnight. But, by then, the slapdash way in which Hitler had planned his strategy and his economy began to count. Not enough tanks had been made to replace losses, and Guderian's six hundred had declined to fifty. There had been nearly 750,000 casualties since June and only 450,000 replacements; in aircraft, the story was much the same. In any case, German supply lines ran only to Smolensk, and Guderian had only thirty miles of fuel. Besides, the autumn mud and, still more, the blizzards of winter found the Germans unprepared. "Do not bother me with this talk about how difficult it is to supply our troops in winter. There will be no winter campaign," Hitler had said. In the snow, German troops froze; they lacked camouflage uniforms, warm underclothing, socks, skis — everything. In the mud of thaw, high roads became quagmires and vehicles skidded if they went too fast or stuck if they went too slowly. The fact was that Bock had overplayed his hand even in "Typhoon," for the Russians, who had organized their war economy more sensibly, fielded more and better-equipped troops in the Moscow theater and elsewhere as well. Even before the real winter began, the German attack had come to a halt. Then, in mid-November, with the snows and the terrible cold building up, there was little chance that they would succeed. Bock was obstinate: "the last battalion will decide the issue." Hitler demanded to know when he could ceremonially enter Moscow. Halder issued fatuous orders to Guderian for a sweeping advance north, east, and south. The reality lay in the 1,360 heavy industrial plants that the Russians had evacuated to the center of their country in the first three months of war, and in the thirty infantry divisions that they brought in from Siberia. They were producing as many planes as in June, one-third more (and superior) tanks, and three times as many guns. German industry was producing, if anything, rather less than in June. By 4 December, the Germans reached within twenty miles of Moscow. But they had run out of steam. Zhukov then was ready with a counteroffensive, for which he had husbanded his resources. It began the next day.

Zhukov's attack came together with crises north and south. On 29 November, a Russian counterattack had won back Rostov; similarly, the Tikhvin salient, and the direct threat to Leningrad, collapsed in the same period. The Russians had prepared for the cold, and the Germans had not. Fires had to be lit under tanks to get their engines going. Telescopic sights would not work. Rifles jammed. German locomotives had their pipes outside the engine, and these froze. The Russians also suffered, but not nearly as much. From 5 December 1941 until February 1942, the Germans had the first real setback they had encountered in the war. It was a measure of Hitler's qualities that they overcame it; a measure again, that they had to undergo it.

In the days after 5 December, Russian troops penetrated the thin German lines in several places. Their cavalry even reached out toward Smolensk and Vyazma; they relieved Tula, to the southwest of Moscow, and threatened Guderian's lines at Oryol and to the south. By mid-month there was crisis everywhere, and fresh Russian offensives were being built up to relieve the attackers in the center. The German generals began to complain. Rundstedt, in the south, said that the only answer must be to pull back to the starting line of June 1941. Brauchitsch finally suffered a complete nervous breakdown and was dismissed. Guderian and Hoepner, who retreated without authority, were summarily dismissed. So was Count Sponeck, who failed in the eastern Crimea. Leeb, of Army Group North, fell under Hitler's ax; so, for a time, did Bock. Five army and thirty-five corps commanders were also dismissed. Behind them all stood Hitler, who on 16 December simply ordered that there were to be no retreats: "By personal intervention of commanders, senior officers, and subalterns, the troops are to be compelled to offer fanatical resistance in their existing positions, without regard for enemy breakthroughs to flank or rear. Only with such tactics can we win the time that is necessary for us to obtain the reinforcements from home and from the west that I have ordered."

To some, this was Hitler's finest hour. He himself took over the command of the army from Brauchitsch on 19 December, and he took a characteristic view of the task: "Anyone can give out a few tactical orders, but a commander in chief's work is to inspire in a national-socialist sense." He would himself take the telephone to speak to beleaguered commanders in snowy wastes, in temperatures that were sometimes as low as −68 Centigrade; and the commanders responded. The German defense was based on "hedgehogs" — positions constructed around vital nodal points in the communications network, without which Russian offensives would soon have to stop. These points might be surrounded; but they could be supplied from the air. Kaluga, Rzhev, Oryol, and Kursk in the central region, Demyansk and Kholm south of Leningrad, and Taganrog and Belgorod in the south were fortresses that stayed the Russian advance. Zhukov tried to break off the two arms that marked the limit of German progress toward Moscow. They were, in the end, evacuated, but the effort cost many Russian lives and did not cause irreparable damage to the Germans, whose new lines to the rear the Russians could not breach.

By mid-January, Army Group Center had had to go back roughly a hundred miles, more in some places. But the Russians could not advance even to Vyazma and Bryansk. There were large salients in Center's line, at Sukhinichi and Rzhev, from which the Germans might again, one day, debouch on Moscow. On the Leningrad front, the Soviet counteroffensives had failed to wipe out such a salient as Demyansk, where one hundred thousand men were supplied from the air until May, when they were relieved. Jodl said of Hitler in this period that "I really admired him then, when his faith and energy brought the tottering eastern front to a stop, for otherwise there could have been an 1812." Hitler later said to Speer, "There were whole days when my nerves were on edge. Almost everyone collapsed, there were only a few who fought with me. Night and day without sleep I had to think, how can I close this or that gap, what can I do, what should happen, because I knew that any retreat would mean the fate of Napoleon. That we got through that winter was only because of the troops' courage and my fanatical will to hold out, whatever the cost."

Even so, he had had to suspend the "Halt-Order" in mid-January and the German army had, for the first time, suffered a considerable defeat. Certainly, the Russians had been fought to a standstill by the end of January; but they were planning new offensives for the spring. Moreover, Germany had acquired the most formidable enemy of all: the United States.

Since the fall of France, President Roosevelt had done what he could to help the anti-German side. His hands were tied by his country's neutrality and also for some time by laws that prevented the sale of weaponry except for cash. He had gradually circumvented these; and, in the autumn of 1940, his warships were being used to protect British ships in the Atlantic. Almost as a separate matter, an American quarrel was pursued with Japan, Hitler's associate since 1937 and ally since 1940. This quarrel flared up into war early in December 1941, when the Japanese attacked the American Pacific Fleet at Pearl Harbor and put much of it out of action. Great Britain declared war on Japan at the side of the United States. Perhaps Hitler might have declared war on Japan as well, in an effort to curry American favor, with appeals against the "Yellow Peril." Instead, he decided that Japanese help would be worthwhile in his war against Russia and Great Britain; and he also knew that, whether war was formally declared or not, American industry and naval power would be at Great Britain's disposal. He too declared war on the United States; the greatest gift he could have made to Roosevelt, who then had an unshakable argument against the isolationists. It would, of course, take some time for American mobilization to become effective. Perhaps, as Hitler argued, a country divided by racial problems and ruled by Jews would be inefficient in war. At all events, he had a real world war on his hands. It would be war to the death. "If the German people is not ready to fight, good — it might as well disappear."

10

The New Order

DEFEAT AT MOSCOW exposed the weaknesses of Hitler's Reich. Outwardly, it was strong and ordered. In reality, it was flashy and self-indulgent, incapable of the sacrifices of comfort that were necessary for a proper war effort. German soldiers might fight skillfully and bravely before Moscow. But the system that sent them there could not supply weaponry or even troops, and could not plan with efficiency until its enemies forced it to do so.

Although Hitler paraded himself as a popular ruler, he was always worried about this. He needed constant success, he thought, and he did not want to place too heavy a burden on the Germans. He disliked rationing, and would have preferred to appeal to people's sense of fair play (though of course only in Germany). Rations remained, in any case, very high, partly from looted goods. Taxes, equally, remained quite low. Even Goering, who was supposed to plan the war economy, opposed closure of civilian factories. He explained that if the workers could not spend their money on consumer goods, there would be inflation; and inflation would mean the end of everything. German output of consumer goods was hardly dented by the war, between 1939 and 1942. In 1941 their value reached a peak, at 14 trillion marks. In 1943 the economy was still producing 12,000 tons of wallpaper and 4,800 tons of hair oil at a time when the British had cut consumer goods to the bone.

It was a similar story with the labor force. Contrary to familiar notions, the economy was not militarized at all. Women, for instance, were discouraged from taking employment, and to the very end there were fewer working women in Germany than in 1918. Even in 1944, there were still 3.5 million male clerks at work; large numbers of others found themselves safe jobs in the administration or in some Party employment. Thus, there were twice as many Germans "directing" the activities of British traitors as there were British traitors; the *Luftwaffe* supported such an enormous ground staff that in the end *Luftwaffe* divisions were set up to give it something to do. The multiplication of separate, conflicting, and overlapping German authorities in occupied countries was such that even well-meaning collaborators did not know where to begin. Some of the authorities would try to collaborate, but others preferred to exploit. In 1943, for instance, German machinery went to France, while the French workers for whom it was meant were drafted to Germany. The French aircraft industry, which had produced thousands of planes before the war, produced twelve hundred in all in 1943.

In the first years of the war, Hitler made next to no effort to alter the economy. On the contrary, he ran its military element down. The *Luftwaffe* best exemplified this:

Aircraft Production 1939–1943

	1939	1940	1941	1942	1943
Germany:	8,300	10,200	11,800	15,400	24,800
Great Britain:	7,900	15,000	20,100	23,700	26,500
U.S.S.R.	10,100	10,600	15,700	25,400	35,000

Even within the military sector, matters were not well arranged. German aircraft production depended on teams of skilled workmen, competing with each other in producing a single aircraft each. No one had any notion of introducing "flow-methods," in which semiskilled workers would concentrate, at a moving belt, on a single operation. Even in 1943, apprenticeship in an aircraft firm took four years, because apprentices were required to know all the operations involved in building an aircraft. The result would be an aircraft that had more polish than that of any other country; but in wartime circumstances, this was simply a luxury.

The *Luftwaffe* planners did not really know what to do. Theoretically, Goering was in charge. But, as the war went on, he grew, by his own confession, "sick to death of the whole business." He visited the Air

Ministry once a week, and spent much of his time in his fabulous manor house at Karinhall, devising ever more gorgeous uniforms, taking morphine, or playing with his enormous toy train. His chief lieutenants were not much better. Ernst Udet, a stunt flyer, confessed to Goering on appointment as chief of staff that he knew nothing about manufacturing. Goering replied, "That's all right, I only want your name." Cigar salesmen, film stars, drug addicts proliferated in this ministry; there was a great gulf between the fighters and the technicians, who at one stage were forbidden to undertake journeys to the front line and had to find out what they wanted to know by writing privately. Not surprisingly, the affairs of this ministry went into inextricable confusion. Too many aircraft types were produced, and research was pursued without liaison: there were seventeen different research establishments, quite apart from those supported by private firms. Yet the *Luftwaffe* took large sums of money and applied for a huge quota of scarce and important metals. Udet thought that an aircraft weighed on average eighteen thousand pounds: in reality, the Me-109 weighed four thousand pounds — Udet had taken the weight of a fully loaded four-engine bomber (Ju-88) as standard. Large quantities of aluminum were therefore sent to the producers, who, in the notorious case of Messerschmitt's factory at Kempten, used it to make ladders for vineyards.

It was beyond Goering to effect much change here, and the Air Ministry became demoralized. Udet and Jeschonnek, who was also responsible for fighters, killed themselves under the strain. A spy ring, the "Red Orchestra," formed in Goering's ministry to work for the Russians. Corruption was such that there were regular imprisonments. The kernel of the whole problem was that no one really knew whether the system was a socialist one or not. Goering would perhaps have liked to centralize everything and operate the kind of economy that Stalin ran, which, during the war, he sometimes held up as a model. The private manufacturers, and many of the officials, naturally disagreed. Hitler himself was too busy to come to terms wiith such a great problem, and it was not solved until too late, in 1942–1943. Meanwhile, the *Luftwaffe*'s numbers remained below establishment: in December 1941, 2,561 of a supposed 4,347; and in September 1942, 3,767 out of 5,068. It was an important factor behind the German halt at Moscow.

Hitler's exploitation of conquered Europe was also thoroughly inefficient. Behind the goose-stepping parades down the Champs Élysées and the sinister, black-and-silver-uniformed Gestapo men there was fabulous disorganization. Some Germans wished to collaborate; others, to exploit; a great many of them were there to escape conscription, as with the officials of the Arado air firm, which maintained five separate liaison offices in Paris for five French air factories, quite apart from the ministry's own personnel. These agencies did not work together, and they had no way of obtaining what they wanted from home, because, there, disorganization was not much less. Unoccupied Hungary supplied much more bauxite than before the war; occupied Yugoslavia and Greece produced much less. At times, the occupation authorities would anticipate the Common Market; at other times, they would operate a straightforward robber-economy. The German people were quite well supplied with food and looted consumer goods in this way, but their war economy received little help.

It was in occupied Russia that the confusion was worst. Some of Hitler's lieutenants thought of helping the lesser peoples of Russia toward dignified semi-independence, with reliance upon Germany. The army usually acted sympathetically toward nationality movements in the Ukraine; it promoted the cause of the anti-Communist General Vlasov and allowed him to recruit a "Free Russian Force" among the prisoners of war and émigrés. Rosenberg, a Baltic German and old Nazi, was put in charge of the "Ministry of the East," and he, too, tended to favor the lesser peoples. But his subordinates, on the whole, did not. Koch, Gauleiter of East Prussia, was put in charge of the occupied Ukraine, and he behaved according to a maxim that Hitler himself heartily endorsed: the peoples of the East respect only force. Ukrainian culture was closed down; priests were persecuted, and peasants were confined in collective farms. Great brutality was used against the populace, particularly the Jews. Perhaps, had the Germans behaved more intelligently, they might have converted the non-Russian peoples to their cause. As it was, the number of partisans increased by the month, and tracking them down involved a considerable military effort. Vlasov's "Free Russian Force" was persecuted, and it found its only serious military function in western Europe. To this day, German officers who were involved with Vlasov regard his movement, perhaps with exaggeration, as the great "might-have-been" of the war. Hitler himself regarded all of the eastern peoples with suspicion. He endorsed the interpretation of 1918, that Germany would have done better in occupied Russia had her men been more brutal — shooting was, he thought, the only argument that was understood in those parts. It was certainly the only argument that Hitler himself understood.

If the Nazis could not be constructive in occupied Europe, they could at least, in the name of order, be extremely destructive. In 1942, Hitler set himself to extinguish the Jews of Europe. Auschwitz, the great concentration camp in southern Poland where millions of Jews were killed by gassing or forced labor, is thus the outstanding monument to Hitler's Germany.

Even so, we do not really know what Hitler's part was in this work. Hitler had always been evasive when he talked of solutions to the Jewish question, although, by the later 1930s, emigration of Jews was the favored answer. In January 1939 he promised the Jews, in a public speech, that if war broke out because of their activities, it would end in "the annihilation of the Jewish race in Europe." However, when war did break out, many different solutions were tried before "the Final Solution" of gassing all of Europe's Jews was put into effect. The Jews of western Europe were, for a time, left alone; those of the Reich were still allowed to emigrate (and of the 375,000 Jews left there, 165,000 remained in 1941); those of Poland were herded into ghettos in 1940 and 1941. In each of these cases, persecution went on. It ranged from the dumping of German Jews from Stettin in occupied Poland to the prohibition on Jews' keeping pet budgerigars in Berlin, on the grounds that the birds would use up birdseed that should have been kept for "Aryan" birds.

It was the Jews of occupied Russia that had the harshest fate in this period. Hitler was always deterred, in his handling of the Jewish question in Europe, by what the western powers might think. Up to December 1941, when the Americans entered the war, his persecution of German Jews was limited. This was not the case in Russia. In March 1941, Hitler issued his "Commissar order," in which he demanded the execution of Bolshevik commissars, gypsies, political enemies, "and all Jews." In the rear of the armed forces, in June 1941, were four *Einsatzgruppen*, or mobile security forces, divided into *Einsatzkommandos*. These groups consisted of up to a thousand men, volunteers from the German police force, the armed SS formations, or the *Sicherheitsdienst* (Security Section of the SS empire), and they were controlled by Heydrich and Himmler, heads of the Gestapo and the SS. The army authorities protested at the atrocities, but they were overruled by Hitler; and in some cases they even supported the *Einsatzgruppen* because these kept down the Soviet partisans. In 1941 and 1942 these groups went ahead. In February 1942, *Einsatzgruppe A* in the Ukraine reported, with that mania for exactitude that distinguished the SS even at its most animal, that it had executed "1,064 commissars, 56 partisans, 653 mental cases, 44 Poles, 28 Russian prisoners of war, 5 gypsies, 1 Armenian and 136,421 Jews." The pattern of these executions had usually been simple enough. The Germans would enter a village, recruit some anti-Soviet local help, and invade the Jewish quarter, burning the houses and shooting their inhabitants, down to the last child. In larger towns like Kiev, the Jewish population would be rounded up, forced to undress, dig their graves, and wait until an SS man came to shoot them in the back of the neck or until machine guns were used.

These methods were not very efficient; and they also had the disadvantage of revolting some of the SS men involved, who became lachrymose drunks. In the summer of 1941, gassing was tried instead of shooting: the victims would be herded into a van, to which the motor's exhaust would be connected until the people were all dead. This method had been tried, following suggestions by Bouhler, of Hitler's private office, and Brack, his doctor, against the mentally sick and handicapped of Germany itself at the very start of the war. The Nazis believed that Germany had lost the First World War because she had been insufficiently ruthless: food had been wasted on such lives as these. From September 1939, the "T4" section of Himmler's empire had been engaged in gassing these unfortunates: over seventy thousand were killed, and the process was stopped only because religious leaders in northwestern Germany protested after a few months. Now, the "T4" men could be employed in the east. There, too, were "useless mouths" who, if fed, would only be hostile to Germany.

In December 1941 these methods were practiced for the first time on the Jews of Poland. By then, various other expedients for coping with the Jewish question had failed. There had been a plan to send the Jews to Madagascar, of which Bouhler saw himself as governor, but that fell through when it became obvious that the British would sink the German ships carrying the Jews out. Another scheme had been promoted by Himmler in 1940, for concentration of Jews in the Lublin region of central Poland, around the town of Nisko. For some months, Jews from central Europe were simply dumped there under the control of the SS chiefs Krüger and Globočnik. They were not housed properly, or fed. They became disease-ridden; and although Frank, the governor-general of Poland, welcomed the appearance of typhus among Jews, he knew that it would soon affect everyone else. Besides, food was scarce and he persuaded Hitler to stop the dumping of German Jews in his territory. Some other answer had to be found.

According to the commandant of Auschwitz, Hoess, who was captured at the end of the war and who made a lengthy confession, it was in midsummer 1941 that Himmler told him, in the greatest secrecy, that the *Führer* had decided to exterminate the Jews. A great camp was built at Auschwitz. Its initial purpose was to hold Poles and Russians, but it was adapted to take Jews. Hoess believed that the existing methods of gassing were inadequate; he preferred to use a prussic-acid poison, Zyklon B, which was commonly used in Germany as a pesticide. Experimentation with it proved to be successful in December. Hitler's knowledge of all this is not established by documents until October 1943. The whole business was conducted with a great deal of secrecy, and Hitler himself seldom spoke of it even to intimates like Speer. It had begun at the suggestion of SS officers in the east, men like Globočnik or Wirth who sought to establish themselves in the hierarchy. Himmler promoted it, and he favored killing Jewish children as well, for otherwise they would grow up to be enemies of Germany — a point that his subordinate, the *Einsatzgruppe* leader Ohlendorf, was to explain to Allied judges at Nuremberg after the war as if it were self-evident. It is inconceivable that Hitler did not know what was happening, even if he was not immediately responsible for the suggestion of the Final Solution.

By January 1942 a compromise was hammered out between the many Germans who wanted to use the Jews' labor (they included the competent army authorities) and those who wished to exterminate the Jews. A conference between various ministries was held at a house on the Wannsee near Berlin on 20 January. The minutes were taken by Eichmann, head of the Gestapo's Jewish emigration office; and we know more about these events from the confession of Eichmann after his trial by the Israelis. Officially, the conference dealt with legal matters — who would count as a Jew. It decided that Jews should be deported (by Eichmann and his lieutenants) to camps in Poland and Russia. Those who could work, would work; those who could not would receive "the logical treatment," that is, they would be gassed. After the conference, Hydrich drank — which he never usually did — and displayed "an old North German custom" of alternately dancing on the table and the chairs.

Treblinka, Sobibór, Betiec, and Majdanek were set up as death camps pure and simple. Work places, with killing arrangements close by, were established in Minsk, Riga, Vilna, and elsewhere. At Auschwitz, there was a death camp (the Polish name of which was Germanized to "Birkenau") and an industrial site ("Monowitz"). Jews from the ghettos of Poland were sent to the camps in regular lots from spring 1942 onward — first the elderly, the women and children and the sick, and then able-bodied men. At the same time, Jews from Germany's allied countries, Slovakia and Romania, were sent to Poland, at least until mid-1942, when the Vatican, which knew what was happening, intervened. In the west, SS officers chased Jews, although passive resistance, especially in

France and Belgium, proved quite effective in preventing disaster. The whole process went on until November 1944, when Himmler stopped it. After that, malnutrition or exhaustion or pestilence accounted for the rest of the six million lives that European Jewry lost. In his final testament, Hitler encouraged his people "above all, to carry on the fight against world Jewry."

The "Final Solution" was not a popular idea in Germany, and although there were constant rumors (spread by soldiers who had seen "actions" against the Jews in the East) as to what was happening, the story of the death camps was kept surprisingly secret. They were all in the occupied East, not in Germany; and the number of Germans involved was astonishingly small. There were fewer than four thousand men in the *Einsatzgruppen* in Russia. The Warsaw ghetto, containing over half a million people, was guarded by fifty SS men. Even Auschwitz had only two thousand German guards for up to three hundred thousand persons. The Jews had decided to confront Nazism with an attitude that, for them, was virtuous traditionalism: obey, do not provoke, and the crisis will pass. In some notorious cases, cooperation between the ghetto leaders and the Nazis went so far that would-be resisters, such as Vitenberg in Vilna, were handed over by Jews for execution. People simply did not believe that the "Final Solution" would be carried out, in such obvious defiance of economic sense as well as of humanity. That it happened at all illustrated the diabolical nature of Hitler's Germany. With every step toward defeat, Hitler became more, and not less, ruthless. As he said, "the tactic is to burn one's boats. That way one fights harder and more ruthlessly."

From the turn of 1941–1942 onward, the power of the SS therefore grew. By 1944, there were 45,000 Gestapo officials, 65,000 security policemen, 2.8 million ordinary policemen, 40,000 guards for 20 concentration camps and 160 work camps attached to them, and 100,000 security police informers. Heydrich looked forward to "total and permanent police supervision of everyone." Regularly, 15,000 people, other than Jews, were placed in concentration camps from 1939 onward (the bulk of them for economic offenses) and, at the end of the war, they contained 750,000 people. An enormous SS economic empire came into existence, with 40 enterprises worked by slave labor and 150 different factories as well as the concentration camps where men worked at quarries or on construction. Himmler's thirty chief lieutenants, the "Senior SS and Police Chiefs," ran private terrorist regimes in their provinces. Inside Germany, the rule of law collapsed. In April 1942, Hitler decided to close the whole charade down. General Hoepner, dis-

Nuremberg

At the Berlin Motor Show, 1935

A visit to Ruhr industry

Visiting a factory

Hitler with close associates, March 1936

Hitler and the Military

Hitler confers with party bosses

The Dictators, July 1944

missed ignominiously by Hitler, sued the Reich for his pension rights and won his case. Hitler summoned the Reichstag and had it vote that, henceforth, Hitler's order should have the force of law. Then the Reichstag stretched out its arm in the German salute, sang the Nazi anthem, and dispersed forever. The first *Führer* order of the new type retroactively denied Hoepner his pension.

Increasingly, with the defeats, Hitler did not trust his technicians. He had always felt ill at ease with most of them, and he was glad to see the back of the Brauchitschs or the Neuraths, however pliantly they behaved. He promoted his own, ultra-Nazi, element. Heinrich Himmler was, he thought, his most faithful adherent. Accordingly, Hitler gave more and more power to the SS. Military resources were given at an increasing rate to form a separate SS army, the *Waffen-SS,* which rose to over half a million men in June 1944 and almost one million by the end of the war. It was Hitler's elite, and he relied more and more on it. The SS fought for power inside Germany against the Party and the bureaucracy; but outside Germany, it met fewer obstacles. It provided an excellent ladder for "outsiders," men who, in the ordinary course of events, would never have earned serious promotion in Germany in anything else. The leadership of the Gestapo and the SS was stuffed with Austrians like Adolf Eichmann or Ernst Kaltenbrunner; 310,000 men of the *Waffen-SS* in 1944 even came from German stock outside the Reich, the so-called *Volksdeutsche* from Poland, the Baltic, or the Balkans and Hungary. This was Hitler's praetorian guard. Hitler looked to them increasingly after the winter defeats of 1941–1942 to provide the fanaticism and ruthlessness that alone, he believed, could overcome the enemies of Germany.

11

World War

IN POLITICS AND, hitherto, in war, Hitler had been a master strategist. His plans always took many factors into account, and they invariably had what Liddell-Hart called "branches": that is, Hitler could profit, or retreat comfortably enough, whatever their outcome. The campaign of 1940 had been characteristic — at the very least, Ruhr industry would be protected by Hitler's plunge into France and Belgium. His great strength had been that he always kept his enemies guessing. As he had said to Raeder in the summer of 1939, he had three kinds of intention, that known to the world, that known to his intimates, and that known only by him. But in February 1942, Hitler's options began to close. He faced a world war, and there were certain fixed requirements that even Hitler could not escape. The Russian front regularly took the bulk of German manpower — 72 percent of the army's divisions in 1942 and 65 percent in 1943, with between two-fifths and two-thirds of the *Luftwaffe*. Then, Hitler's strategy was inevitably based on keeping allies such as the Finns, the Romanians, and, especially, the Italians in the war. Besides, he was in a hurry, because the strength of the enemy coalition would obviously increase vastly as time went by. At the turn of 1941–1942 Hitler radicalized his war effort. A serious war economy came into existence; the dictatorship in Germany was strengthened; the "Final Solution" was inaugurated. Morally, at any rate, Hitler burned his boats and prepared for a great gamble on victory.

In 1942, he still had many advantages. Although the Americans had entered the war, they had no army to speak of and much of their navy was occupied against the Japanese. It would take them time to produce war matériel, and while they were producing it, they would have less to spare for the British (indeed, under Lend-Lease in this period of the war, the Americans took almost as large a fraction of British output as the British of American). The British themselves were in much better shape than before, but they could not strike hard at Germany proper. Much of their effort was still taken up with defense, this time against German U-boats.

Here was another of Hitler's successes cheaply won. He himself had preferred to concentrate on flashy capital ships, not submarines, and so he had few submarines to use in 1939. Even in 1942, a smaller proportion of steel was being used for submarines than in 1939. The force that was operational on the high seas at any time grew slowly from 22 early in the war, to 50 in 1942, and to 101 in March 1943. In 1940 the British had been weak in escorts for their convoys, and the submarines sank, per month, more ships than the British could replace. Then, with Lend-Lease, American destroyers supplied more escorts, and sinkings decreased. There followed a duel, not unlike that of medieval times, between fortress architecture and siege technique. The British came up with a whole variety of ingenious devices — "Ultra" to crack the German codes; radar beams that the Germans could not detect and that led British planes toward submarines; improved underwater detection; multiple depth charges; and searchlights that could be carried by aircraft. Admiral Doenitz responded by ever more cunning tactics. It was a "silent war," one demanding the highest degree of endurance on both sides. The British won it, in effect, only when they were able to cover the entire Atlantic from the air, which enabled them to detect and sink German submarines operating in the middle. This did not happen until March 1943. Up to then, the western powers had lost 21.5 million tons, and built 16.5 million; thereafter, the U-boats were virtually ineffective. The Atlantic battle, rather than the Battle of Britain, was the real "finest hour" of Churchill's war.

Even so, it was essentially defensive. When the British turned to offensive action, things went wrong for them. A very great proportion of their war effort went into the bombing attacks against Germany from the spring of 1942 onward. The RAF had not really absorbed the lesson that it had itself inflicted upon the Germans in 1940: that bombing attacks on civilian targets merely heightened the other side's war effort and will to win. Of course, Great Britain had to do something against Germany, if only for the Russians' sake, and at that time Churchill's advisers were adamantly against the risks of a military landing in France. Yet bombers, however bravely taken through fighter and flak defenses, could not achieve anything against industrial targets, especially at night. Bombs could not be accurately dropped. A thousand yards was the average error, although, as techniques improved, the distance was reduced to two hundred yards. The British responded to this by pretending that they were attacking industrial targets, whereas in reality they merely wrecked German homes and killed innocents.

From spring 1942, with lulls before and during the great Anglo-American amphibious operations of winter 1942–3 and summer 1944, great bombing raids were conducted against German cities. On 30 May 1942, a "thousand-bomber raid" wrecked six hundred acres of Cologne. In June and July, similar raids struck at the ancient Hanseatic towns of the Baltic coast — Lübeck, Rostock, Hamburg, which had medieval centers that easily could be burned to nothing — causing "fire storms" that caused even the air to burn. This did little damage to German war production, though it is maybe arguable that, had the bombing raids not occurred, production would have been still greater. It is even possible that the bombing attacks caused German production to rise, for they destroyed the civilian economy — shops, banks, schools, and the like — and thereby forced labor from that still inflated sector toward the manufacture of war goods. "Bomber" Harris, rather than Hitler, laid the groundwork for the spurt in German war production that occurred after the early months of 1942. It reached a peak in the summer of 1944, and did not begin to suffer the effects of bombing until the Allies had secured such control of the German skies that they could bomb industrial targets during the day.

Otherwise, British offensive action in 1941 and 1942 had very little effect on Germany. It had been concentrated against the Italians in Africa. It was true that this absorbed Axis shipping and air power, but the Italian soldiers had little stomach for this war; their tanks were obsolete, there commanders did not understand even these, and their sanitation was a potent weapon on the British side. The picture altered in spring 1941 when Hitler sent Rommel with two weak Panzer divisions and a light infantry division. Rommel behaved with dash — using minefields, outflanking maneuvers, he captured supply dumps and dummy tanks with great verve, and converting his antiaircraft gun, the eighty-eight millimeter, into an antitank gun. From spring 1941 the British did badly. Their troops were untrained, their officers were too polite to each other, and "it was regarded as axiomatic that the tanks would not be where they were wanted." Their attacks, "Battleaxe" in June and

"Crusader" in November 1941, failed, with high loss in tank strength.

Despite what the British thought at the time, Hitler was not very interested in the desert war, and he kept Rommel on a logistical shoestring; indeed, Rommel was only there because Hitler wished to keep Italy in the war. However, Rommel's successes in 1941 and 1942 decided Hitler that perhaps a great sweep could be made from the Suez Canal, through the Middle East (with the Vichy French collaborating from their possession in Syria) toward Iraq, where there was smoldering anti-British feeling, and Iran, which would turn pro-German if the Germans approached it. This would come together with a similar vast sweep through southern Russia and the Caucasus.

Hitler had few troops to spare for Rommel, but he could at least send aircraft. Submarines and *Luftwaffe* aircraft were diverted from the Atlantic and Russia (Albert Kesselring, with the Second Air Fleet) and an assault was made on Malta, which acted as a giant aircraft carrier for the British to disrupt Italian and German supplies. Up to then, Rommel had been in a position of almost absurd inferiority to the British. At the time of "Crusader," for instance, he had had nine divisions only, seven of them Italian, and he had faced 700 British modern tanks with 174 Panzer IIIs and 146 Italian tanks that were obsolete; his air strength was half that of the British. Then, in spring 1942, he was given rather more, and British supplies were disrupted by the Axis powers' diversion of strength to the Mediterranean. Even so, when he attacked at Gazala on 26 May, he was still slightly inferior in force. The British were also deceived by their own ingenuity. They could read the ultrasecret German codes, and therefore knew that Hitler and the Italians were telling Rommel to clear up Malta before going on to the desert. Rommel disobeyed, and caught the British by surprise. By 20 June, the port of Tobruk had collapsed and Rommel had taken more prisoners than his own numbers. He reached the Egyptian border and ran up against a strong defensive position at El Alamein. He had then only fifty-five tanks and two thousand German infantry, and was forced to pause. Even so, the British prepared to evacuate Cairo; the debris of burning paper was such that one day was known as "Ash Wednesday." Then the British displayed resilience. A new general, Viscount Montgomery, took charge; the supply lines were again cleared, and Rommel's were interrupted. In August, Rommel's attack was held; by October, a new British attack was planned. Rommel's victories inspired the German public. Yet Hitler knew that, useful as they were, they could not be decisive unless he won the war in Russia outright. It was there that his mental energies were concentrated.

The calamities of winter 1941–1942 had shaken Hitler's confidence. According to Jodl, he began, then, to see that he might be defeated. The strain began to tell on him personally. He had always alternated between periods of exhilaration and periods of cataleptic depression. These alternations worsened. Hitler began to sleep badly; he would lie, hour after hour, listening to the whine of the air conditioning in the concrete compound of Rastenburg, deep in the dreary East Prussian landscape. After a time, he, understandably, tired of his own company. "I can't bear being alone nowadays," he said. The doctors recommended he drink a glass of beer to help him get to sleep; but he was too worried about putting on weight. Instead, he put off the hour of sleep. After dinner, he would sit with his cronies — the secretaries, Bormann, Speer if he were there, an officer or two — and talk. He talked and talked and talked; covering all possible subjects except, curiously, the war, to which he did not allude very often. Bormann, a crafty gangster to whom Hitler appeared to be a scholar, arranged to have the table talk discreetly noted down. Eyes would glaze, heads would be propped up as Hitler rambled over history: "the decline of the Dutch must have been due to their interbreeding with Malays"; "Jesus Christ's father cannot have been a Jew, he was probably a soldier of the Roman garrison"; "the English may have Shakespeare, but otherwise they have produced just barbarians and cowards." Yet the secretaries and SS adjutants or valets rather liked him. He could be kindly; he was extremely affectionate toward his dogs. But Halder, his army chief of staff, disapproved of these doings. Hitler felt uncomfortable under his thin-lipped scrutiny.

But if, in December 1941, Hitler had come to doubt, he recovered a few weeks later. The Russian winter offensives collapsed against well-prepared German lines; there was every sign that, with the return of good weather, the firm soil would once more allow the Germans their tremendous advantage in mobile warfare. The army came back to strength, at just over three million men. In 1942, war production recovered: its value more than doubled over the figures for 1941, rising from $6 billion to $13.8 billion. Aircraft output rose at last, by 50 percent, as the organizers and manufacturers responded to real war. Admittedly, Germany could produce only five hundred tanks per month whereas the Russians could produce one thousand, quite apart from the substantial help they were receiving, at this time, from the British and Americans. But German antitank defenses were good, and German tactics would surely do the rest. Confidence recovered as the last Russian winter offensive came to an end in the slush and mud of the Volkhov front, south of Leningrad. On 28 March, Hitler held a conference.

The conference resulted in "Case Blue," the most fantastic ever made up by Hitler, for it prescribed an offensive in southern Russia toward the Volga, the Caspian, and the Caucasus. Army Group South would be given the bulk of the infantry and two Panzer armies under Hoth and Kleist. The aim was to capture the oil wells of the Caucasus area, which supplied thirty million tons of crude oil per year. In German hands, this would make all the difference. It would allow vast expansion of the German airforce; it would halt Russian mobility altogether. Hitler said, "If I don't get Maikop and Grozny (oil wells) I'll have to stop the war." After that, Hitler would imitate Alexander the Great, sweeping down through central Asia toward India, where there would be a revolt against the British, to link up, overland, with his Japanese allies. To mark the new phase, Hitler shifted to a kind of frontier headquarters at Vinnitsa, in the western Ukraine. There, log cabins were built to house him and his staff. The sun beat relentlessly down; mosquitoes tested everyone's nerves. This was the Hitler who avidly read the works of the German Zane Grey, Karl May, which constituted his chief reading matter in the 1930s.

As had happened before Barbarossa, the Russians began by making Hitler an enormous present. Already, they had lost seven million soldiers (more than in the First World War) and (literally) uncounted thousands of tanks. However, their production had recovered astonishingly quickly, and they came back into the field with a very imposing force of five million to the Germans' two, with four times as many tanks as the Germans had. Stalin had ignored the prudent advice of Zhukov and decided to launch offensives of his own which, he hoped, would profit from the dry ground, the fresh troops, and the Germans' weakness. Three of these were planned — one on the Volkhov, south of Leningrad, one in the Kerch area of the eastern Crimea, and one on the Donets river, toward Kharkov, chief city of the eastern Ukraine.

The Volkhov offensive proved to be a disaster: Andrey Vlasov, the Soviet general who later turned traitor, led off the attack but received feeble flanking support and ran into a trap set up from the German "pocket" at Demyansk. Then, on 8 May, the Russian commander of the Crimea, Mekhlis, carefully gathered his forces for attack from the Kerch peninsula. Manstein, the German commander, had his blow on a Russian force that was already exposed, waiting to attack, and underdeployed for defense. German E-boats floated along an antitank ditch that the Russians had flooded; and Mekhlis, in John Erickson's words, "threw away three armies in a nightmare of confusion and incompetence." Then Manstein turned against the Russian fortress of Sevastopol, which had held out since the late autumn. Two enormous guns, "Karl" and "Dora," each the size of a three-story house and each needing sixty locomotives for traction, threw three-ton projectiles over thirty miles; the fortress fell on 4 July. These disasters knocked out the Russians' northern and southern troops for several months to come.

But the greatest disaster happened at Kharkov. Timoshenko and Golikov, the Russian commanders in the Ukraine, had built up a very large force, almost one million men with three thousand tanks. Timoshenko intended to use a bridgehead over the Donets at Izyum to debouch toward Kharkov, and retake the great industrial and mineral regions of southern Russia. At the same time, Hitler had ordered his soldiers in this area to start their attack on 18 May. It was in fact Timoshenko who began, on 12 May. The German group had only twelve hundred tanks. Friedrich Paulus, who led the Sixth Army on the northern side of the Izyum salient, wished to withdraw, and so did Kleist, whose Panzer army covered the southern side. Halder too hesitated, and so did Bock, who had been brought back from temporary retirement to lead the army group. It was Hitler who held out. Paulus, he said, must hold Kharkov, though he might fall back so as to lead the Russians on; then, with the date of Kleist's attack advanced to 17 May, Kleist would cut into the Russians' flank, where their tanks were exposed to the kind of flat-trajectory, close-range fire that would not fail to knock out even T-34s. Since German Panzer divisions, unlike Russian ones, had a unit of eighty-eight millimeter antitank guns that cooperated well with the tanks, this plan promised success. Kleist attacked the exposed flank and probed deep into the rear of the Izyum salient. Russian coordination among tanks, artillery, infantry, and aircraft proved wanting; Paulus prevented Timoshenko's armor from disrupting Kleist's; 240,000 Russians were caught in the Izyum pocket, and the Germans captured twelve hundred tanks. Then, profiting from the isolation of two armies to east and northeast that this disaster had brought about on the Russian side, Hitler mounted two separate operations, "Wilhelm" and "Fridericus," against them, on 9 and 22 June. Again there were large numbers of prisoners, almost one hundred thousand, with twelve hundred tanks, and the ratio of Russian to German tanks, which had been two to one before, now became one to four.

"Blue," toward the Caucasus, then could begin, on 28 June, against thin Russian forces. The plan had been worked out on 1 June when Hitler visited Bock's headquarters at Poltava and there met the chief commanders — Bock, his chief of staff Sodenstern, Kleist and Ruoff, Weichs, Hoth, and Paulus. From the start, "Blue" really had two objectives — the Caucasus, with its oil wells, and the Volga, around the town of Stalingrad. The great danger for Hitler was that, as his forces moved into the oil regions of the Caucasus, they would have, to the north, a thousand-mile-long flank that could be easily penetrated by the Russians. To obviate this danger, Hitler would try to draw in the Russian forces to certain fixed points on the flank. Voronezh, on the middle Don (just east of the Donets positions already taken) was one; Stalingrad, a large industrial city (which, coincidentally, had Stalin's name), was another. The whole plan was fantastic; but, Hitler's ideas probably gave it its only chance of success.

Success did, however, depend on speed, which in turn depended on tanks. The generals, in Hitler's view, let him down. On the northern side, a German, a Hungarian, an Italian, and a German Panzer army (Hoth) moved, as a group under Weichs, toward the Don at Voronezh. The idea was for these forces to take Voronezh and hold it as a linchpin for the flank. Once the flank was safe, German tanks could then shift rapidly toward the south, to trap the Russians who held the line opposite Paulus; and once these Russians had been dislodged, the German groups would move southeast to threaten encirclement of the Russian front that ran south, to the Sea of Azov, on the river Mius. Bock, who commanded the entire operation, did not see things Hitler's way. He reached Voronezh, the Russians simply retreating there, on 5 July, and kept some of the armor to help him to capture it. The city fell on 7 July, but the bulk of the group's armor had been held there for two days (which Hitler regarded as vital), and so the Russian forces to the south were able to pull out toward the east before it was too late. As Paulus's force moved forward, a further attempt to encircle the retreating Russians (at Millerovo, on the eastern side of the Don) also failed in mid-July. Not many prisoners were taken this time; all that had been achieved was a threat to the rear of the Russian defense to the south, on the Mius, and at Rostov-on-the-Don, gateway to the Caucasus. On 23 July these forces retired from the city. The Germans then could invade the Caucasus. It looked spectacular, on the map, but the realities were different on the ground, and Hitler began to quarrel deeply with his generals.

In the first place, he dismissed Bock, and he divided his forces into two new army groups, A (List) to invade the Caucasus and B (Weichs) to protect the flank by an active maneuver toward the lower Volga. The two operations were known respectively as "Edelweiss" and "Siegfried." For both, there were only sixty-eight divisions, one third of them Romanian, Italian, Hungarian, or Slovak, and of these only seven were motorized, and nine armored. Yet the plan prescribed a vast lengthening of the German front from five hundred miles (Oryol to Taganrog) to almost three thousand (Oryol to Stalingrad to the Caucasus) with extreme lengthening of supply lines. On top of this, Hitler decided to impress his Finnish allies by sending Manstein with the Eleventh Army to the north, to besiege Leningrad ("Operation Northern Lights") with its two enormous guns; and he also withdrew two excellent divisions, the SS *Leibstandarte* (Guard) and *Grossdeutschland* (Greater Germany), to be retrained with armor in the west. Similarly, he let Army Group Center undertake a costly and ineffective attack (at Sukhinichi) and shifted four hundred aircraft to the Mediterranean. All of this makes sense only if Hitler were convinced that the Russians had been so badly defeated in May and June that they would never recover. True, it took them some months to repair the damage, but they gained something more worthwhile than any tactical victory: meanwhile Stalin perceived that he must let his technicians try their hands seriously, and from then on he let the Zhukovs, Vasilevskys, Konievs, and Rokossovskys manage things instead of his ancient, bullheaded cronies. The days of the giant Russian blunders were over.

By contrast, Hitler began to part from his technicians. His relations with them had been good enough in his early years in power, because he had accepted more or less everything they said, though sometimes he had to mediate when (as with Guderian and Blomberg in matters of armored warfare) they disagreed. In the later 1930s he had taken a more active part in their deliberations; his technical knowledge impressed many of them and his excellent memory enabled him to reel off statistics about American coal production, artillery calibers, thickness of armor plating on ships or tanks. In the very early period of the war, he had relied on Brauchitsch, Halder, Keitel, or Jodl; he had been deferential toward men like Bock; he had encouraged Manstein. The fall of France seems to have turned his head, as well it might; and his greatest achievement to date, the holding of such an enormous stretch of Soviet territory, had also occurred despite, rather than because of, the advice of his generals. They had wanted to retreat from Moscow, and Hitler had decided to stay put. He had turned out to be right then, and was again in May and June 1942, when the generals recommended different tactics for meeting Timoshenko's offensive. It was not surprising that Hitler saw himself as a military genius and that he found men like Keitel or Paulus, commander of the Sixth Army, agreeing with this. Halder was discountenanced.

The tug between "Edelweiss" into the Caucasus, which on the whole the generals favored, and "Siegfried" toward Stalingrad, which Hitler wished to promote, now became intolerable, for the force was not enough to cover both. There was, in Army Group A for "Edelweiss," one armored group, Kleist's First Panzer Army, as well as an infantry army, Ruoff's Seventeenth, which moved over Rostov and the Kerch Strait — the mouth of the Sea of Azov — to invade the Kuban area north of the Caucasus mountains. Would that armor be enough? The generals wanted another armored force, Hoth's Fifth Panzer Army, to join in. It was far to the north — indeed, it was on the northern side of Paulus's Sixth Infantry Army. The generals decided that it should be brought southwest. In doing so, it crossed Paulus's line of advance toward Stalingrad, and then ran into Kleist's Panzer Army as it came east from Rostov.

Inevitably, there was a traffic jam on the few roads and the entire central force was immobilized for ten days, until the beginning of August. Besides, Hitler really wanted Hoth's armor to help the drive toward Stalingrad. There followed an intense, bitter dispute in the hideous huts of Hitler's Vinnitsa headquarters. On 23 July, Hitler screamed at Halder for causing these delays; tempers worsened as the facts of the jam became plain. Hitler decided that Hoth's armor should move toward the east; but the generals managed things so that fuel which should have gone to Hoth and enabled him to push on to Stalingrad when that city was still weak, went instead to Kleist's tanks. Then the order was countermanded by Hitler, and it was Kleist's turn to be held up for lack of fuel. Halder whined into his diary: "The situation is becoming intolerable. There is no room for serious work. This 'leader' is pathological, just reacting to impressions of the moment." Hitler dismissed his generals as "a bunch of sausages." "Blue" was a month old, and where was the decision?

Still, the Russians were crippled, especially in the Don–Volga area, and in August they simply fell back. Weichs's army group held the lengthening northeastern flank, roughly along the Don downriver from Voronezh, while its chief element, Paulus's Sixth Army, with Hoth on his right, moved east over the Don to cross the strip of land between it and the Volga, and came up to Stalingrad at the end of August. The three Russian armies against him had only four hundred tanks, one hundred seventy-two fighters, and twenty divisions (of an original thirty-eight) with only two thousand men apiece. The local Russian commander, Andrei Ivanovich Yeremenko, did retain two bridgeheads over the Don, at Kletskaya and Serafimovitch, which Weichs sealed off with Romanian troops. On 1 September, Paulus began the siege of Stalingrad.

On 26 July, List's army group crossed the river Manych, which acts as boundary between Europe and Asia. He was to take Baku, the great oil-refining city on the Caspian, and the Black Sea ports of Novorossiysk, Tuapse, and Batum. There was some collaboration among the local Cossacks and multifarious Caucasian peoples, many of whom had obscure but deeply felt grievances against each other. On the plains, German progress was good. Krasnodar, Maikop, and Grozny duly fell on 9 August, although the Russians had put concrete over the oil wells to prevent the Germans from exploiting them. By early September, List's group had run into one geographical and logistical problem after another. The mountains were far too high; the mountain tracks were far too narrow; the supply line, to Rostov, was simply too far away; on the Black Sea the Germans could not use water transport because the Soviet navy interrupted it.

Although the Russians had lost four thousand tanks, their production was such that the numbers would be made up again by the end of the year; and their army in the Caucasus was still being supplied through the Caspian port of Astrakhan. List's group, on its four ox tracks, could only inch forward at seven miles per week. The Germans sent a team to plant the swastika on Mount Elburz, the highest peak, and they also came within sight of Astrakhan. Then they virtually stopped, apart from minor advances along the Black Sea coast. Hitler raged. Why had List delayed? Why had he not transported the Romanian divisions from the Crimea to the Caucasus in time? Why had the generals given such priority to Army Group A when the decisive maneuver ought to have been that of Paulus and Army Group B? The Russians' link between the Caucasus and the center must be snapped, and that could be done at Stalingrad. Jodl was sent off on a journey to see List. He came back and reported, quite fairly, that List was making the best of an appallingly difficult job. Hitler refused to shake hands with him, and when Jodl defended Halder, Hitler stormed at him: "Never in all my life did I experience such an outburst of rage from any human being." By early September, Hitler was refusing to eat with the generals, and had meals with his cook instead. In fact, she turned out to have some Jewish blood, and so Hitler, though he liked her, had her replaced.

From 7 September, moods worsened. Hitler and the generals now disputed as to the record: who had decided what? Halder maintained that he was blameless. Hitler's answer was to move into the conference hut at Vinnitsa eight typists, who were to take down every word that was spoken there. The record filled five hundred pages every day. That way, at least, Hitler could point to concrete evidence of his genius. The daily report was now made, not in the map room, but in Hitler's own

quarters; and increasingly, Hitler kept the company of his adoring SS
adjutants. Finally, on 24 September, Halder was replaced as chief of
staff by a forty-seven-year-old general, Kurt Zeitzler. He was a man of
bustling energy, who owed his rise to his use of wheeled craft, with sails,
that were used in the winter of 1941–1942 to defeat the Russians by
surprise on the frozen Sea of Azov. He stood up to Hitler, not in the
underhand, resentful way of Halder, but man to man. Hitler respected
his judgment. Later, he had Halder put in prison.

By then, with the Caucasus operation running down, Stalingrad had
become the main front. When Paulus attacked, the defense was very
weak; it continued to be weak, because Zhukov, who then had charge of
the entire operation, wished to build up his forces on the long, exposed
Don flank while the main German forces were engaged in Stalingrad.
General Chuikov, the defending commander, was therefore told to make
do with one hundred thousand men to the Germans' four hundred thousand, and with similar inferiorities in most types of weaponry. The
Germans had five times as many tanks, and twice as many guns as
Chuikov.

However, tanks (as was shown again and again) were not built for
attacks on a town. Rubble held them up, and as they went slowly
forward over it, they could be knocked out by antitank artillery —
bazookas were then introduced into all of the armies. Besides, Chuikov
could be supplied by ferry over the river Volga, and though many of the
boats were sunk, enough ammunition did get through. From 1 September to 18 November Paulus was on the attack, in four great offensives.
There was fighting of extreme ferocity around certain key points — the
Barrikady artillery factory, the southern railway station, the Red October factory, and the "tennis racket" (as the railway junction was
known). By 8 November, all but a tenth of the city had fallen, while the
Russians held on, in separated pockets, at various points along the
river's edge. The battlefield was a wilderness of twisted metal, rubble
from the buildings, burned-out tanks, and hollow facades; underneath it,
there was furious digging as sappers of both sides mined and counter-
mined, connecting cellars, sewage systems, and tunnels.

Hitler had always said that he would not let his army be involved in a
great, fixed slogging match such as Verdun had been in the First World
War. But, he did just that. He made Stalingrad a matter of personal
prestige. Of course, for much of the time, he was far from alone in
thinking that it would easily fall: in October, Goering had made a
boastful speech at the Sportpalast in Berlin, and on 8 November Hitler
was told (and he repeated it in a public speech commemorating the

putsch of 1923) that the city had fallen. The army's intelligence service had said that the Russians had no more reserves; it also was sure that there would be no Russian offensive in that area. By early November, as winter threatened, there were alarms. Paulus only needed to look over his shoulder, at the stalemate in the Caucasus and the long, vulnerable flank on the Don, to appreciate the dangers of his position. He himself wished to have the front withdrawn to the Don and Donets. So did Weichs. Hitler was adamant: no withdrawal. After all, this method had worked in December 1941. Paulus trusted Hitler. Like many Nazis, he was a man of insecure social standing in a very class-bound profession. Hitler gave him a fixed point; and had not Hitler proved thoroughly right, in mid-May, at the time of the Izyum affair, when Paulus had argued a different case? Paulus suppressed his own doubts and those of his corps commanders as well. The battle inside Stalingrad went on.

While it went on, Zhukov built up an enormous force on the Don flank, of nine hundred tanks, a million men, and 1,115 aircraft to a German and allied force less than half its strength. "Operation Uran," as the Russian attack was called, depended upon exploitation of the Don bridgeheads that had been retained in August at Kletskaya and Sera-fimovitch. There would be a subsidiary attack south of Stalingrad from the Volga. Both attacking forces hit weak troops — for the most part, Romanians. These men often fought bravely, but their tanks were light, and in any case they had suffered an unforeseeable misfortune: to keep the cold out, they had been dug in, and their bases had been packed with straw. Field mice got at the straw, and nibbled the electrical wiring as well. The initial Russian onslaught on the Third Romanian Army was therefore met with only twenty tanks, and the Germans also had only 594 air-worthy planes, 141 of them fighters, in this area.

Not surprisingly, there was immediate disaster. On 19 November, Konstantin Rokossovsky attacked on the Don flank; on the following day Nikolai Vatutin attacked from the other wing. The Romanians on both sides scattered. The German Heim's Panzer corps disintegrated in the melee. The only operational reserve at hand, Mellenthin's Panzer corps, was also rudely pushed out of the way. The Russians' further progress depended upon their seizing the Don bridge at Kalach, in the path of the two attacking groups. Captured German tanks were used in a ruse which caused the defenders of this bridge not to demolish it in time. Vatutin and Rokossovsky met up on 22 November, and Paulus was encircled by 250,000 men.

What next? In Hitler's view, this was not a unique crisis. After all, German groups had been cut off before, and had been supplied from the air, to be relieved some months later. This was what he had in mind now. Zeitzler and Jodl both thought, though maybe with greater hesitancy than they later made out, that there should be an immediate withdrawal while Paulus still had fuel and ammunition and before the Russian encirclement grew too tight. Against that counted, first, the loss of prestige, and, second, — and much more important — the fact that almost one million men in Army Group A would be cut off in the Caucasus if the Russians acted quickly enough. If Stalingrad held out, then there could be a relatively orderly withdrawal from the mountains; indeed, if it held out well, then there need not even be such a withdrawal at all. Hitler gambled again. He told Paulus to stay put, and he ordered a relief attack to be mounted.

Manstein, whom Hitler trusted, was put in charge of a special army group, Don, to organize this. Hoth's Panzer army stood to the south, and two hundred tanks were made ready for a counterstroke on 12 December. It was quite cunningly thought up. But it broke down, at Kotelnikovo, still forty miles from Paulus. In mid-December, the Italian Eighth Army, neighbor, to the north, of the beaten Romanians, was attacked, and it collapsed, causing poor Manstein to withdraw some of Hoth's troops to support its line. There then was a threat that the Russians would reach Rostov before the Caucasus troops could withdraw. By Christmas day they were only thirty miles from it. Manstein begged Hitler to give the order for evacuation.

Hitler bowed to necessity on 29 December, though with immense reluctance. The Caucasus forces, generally, then under Kleist, were told that they had better withdraw. At least, there was some sense in keeping Stalingrad. Goering promised that the *Luftwaffe* would be able to supply it if it held out, like the Demyansk pocket a year before, until the end of the winter. Hitler "thumped the table and said, 'we are not budging from the Volga'." He told Bormann that it would be better to conscript the fifteen-year-olds and fight on: "It would still be better for them to die fighting in the east than for us to lose this war and see them tortured and sent into slavery."

Paulus had warned Hitler that his ammunition was running low. One of his corps commanders, Seydlitz-Kurzbach, undertook a retreat from exposed positions without authorization. Hitler ignored these signs: so long as Stalingrad held out, with the swastika still flying from its highest building, the Russians would be provoked, almost from empty prestige motives, to concentrate against it. So they did. Seven Soviet armies, with 107 brigades or divisions (and at one stage, 143) were pinned on the Stalingrad perimeter. True, they were also attacking on a three-hundred-mile front along the Don, and they broke the Second Hungarian Army in mid-January near Voronezh. But they were not able to break through effectively toward the Black Sea and the Sea of Azov, where they could have cut off the retreat from the Caucasus. Just north of Rostov, brilliantly led mixed German forces under Hollidt and Fretter-Pico exploited the Russians' supply problems and kept the road through Rostov open.

Throughout January, a retreat was managed from the Caucasus, in which three-quarters of a million men were evacuated, together with many refugees. Mackensen's First Panzer Army retreated over four hundred miles, with eighteen-horse teams pulling the heavy artillery along mountain tracks. Twenty-five thousand hospital cases were evacuated; the whole group lost only 100 guns and 226 men. There were troubles elsewhere. Army Group Center had not done well; Army Group North had lost at Velikiye Luki in November, and a small gap had been prised in the besieging forces around Leningrad early in 1943. By 23 January, Army Group North had 3 tanks, Army Group Center 167, and the southern groups together 324. That the Russians did not capture all of these groups in a "super-Stalingrad" had much to do with Paulus's keeping so many of them occupied on the Volga.

But Paulus's own fate was terrible. The *Luftwaffe* could not supply him properly. One thousand Ju-52 transports would have been needed, and there were only 750 in the entire air force. *Luftwaffe* production had recovered, in 1942, but the types produced were standard, unimaginative ones; the bolder experiments had, so far, been a story of crashes and delays. Russian aircraft, and the cold, interfered with proper supply, and Paulus also lost the only good airstrip at Gumrak. Only ninety tons of the daily five hundred needed were in fact dropped; Manstein's headquarters at Novocherkassk was a scene of bitter contention among Goering, Richthofen, Jeschonnek, and Milch as to who, of the air force, bore the responsibility. Paulus's forces were then cut in two. Hitler promoted him to field marshal, assuming no doubt that it would inspire Paulus to die in the last ditch. But by 30 January, most of his forces had surrendered, and on 2 February the rest followed. One hundred fifty thousand men had been lost, and over one hundred thousand entered Russian captivity, from which only a few thousand ever returned. By early February, the eastern front was set for another huge Russian offensive.

12

The Beginning of the End

"YOU FIND TRUE GREATNESS in the hour of misfortune, like Frederick the Great," Hitler told Zeitzler at this time. The misfortunes in Russia were not the only ones. Things had gone badly elsewhere, particularly in Africa. By mid-November 1942, disaster threatened there as well; that Germany survived for so long thereafter was a measure of Hitler's extraordinary tenacity.

June 1942 had been the peak of success for the Axis. Thereafter, there was decline. The Japanese, fighting their virtually separate war, lost a large part of the aircraft-carrier force at the battle of Midway, and thereafter they were on the defensive as Australian and American forces went from island to island in relentless pursuit. Rommel, in North Africa, had invaded Egypt in that month, though he had been held up in July and August at the El Alamein positions. Now, Montgomery was preparing a counterstroke. Until this was ready, he confined himself to the most prudent of careful defensive actions.

Hitler had given Rommel only a small force of two weak Panzer divisions and a light division; most of his troops were in fact Italians. This investment, slight as it was, prevented the Anglo-Americans from launching a second front in Europe to help the Russians. In 1942, the Americans were full of fight and wished to stage a European invasion that year. The British were much more cautious. They could see the immense difficulties of an amphibious operation — so many ships needed, each carrying far fewer men than could be carried by European railway, so much oil, so great a superiority in the air. Perhaps they overrated the problem. But for better or worse, they decided that an amphibious operation should be risked only when the Germans were already weakened on other fronts. They had, at least in narrow military terms, the chief voice in Europe, and by July 1942 the Americans, who would have liked to invade Europe at once, were overruled. Instead, the resources of the Anglo-American coalition were bizarrely concentrated against French and Italian North Africa. There was to be a landing in French North Africa, after which the German-Italian rear in Tunisia could be threatened; at the same time, Montgomery would attack from Egypt. An enormous force, out of all proportion to the Germans' *Afrikakorps*, was assembled.

Rommel had an immense problem, as well, with supply lines. Malta had not been knocked out, and continued to offer shelter to British convoys through the Mediterranean. Its aircraft also sank Axis shipping and spotted submarines. The withdrawal of German planes back to the Russian front left Malta free to carry on her fateful role. Aircraft from there had made short work of Italian warships in 1940 and 1941. Now they disrupted Rommel's supplies to such an extent that, in August, the British had half a million tons of supplies where Rommel received thirteen thousand.

By mid-October, Montgomery had assembled enormous weight. He attacked the El Alamein lines on 23 October, with 230,000 men to 80,000 (27,000 Germans), 1,440 tanks to 540 (260 German) and 1,500 aircraft to 350. The British Grant tanks were supplemented by Shermans that the Germans could knock out only at very close range. Besides, the German tanks had only three days' issue of fuel instead of thirty. Virtually all British generals had a habit, when they enjoyed vast material superiority, of giving up military ingenuity and relying on crushing force in a somewhat unsubtle way. Montgomery did this too, only, unlike his predecessors, he dealt out his high cards in sensible order. He drove his tanks through narrow corridors opened in the German tank traps, and continued to drive them through until the defense had been worn down. In three days, the British lost 600 tanks, the Germans 150; in effect, this increased the British tank superiority from four to one to eleven to one.

The same method was applied again and again, and Montgomery's casualties were actually higher, as a proportion of combatant strength, than Haig's had been on the Somme in 1916. But he won. By the beginning of November, Rommel had been worn down. He was left with five thousand Germans, twenty-five hundred Italians, and twenty-one tanks. Then, on 8 November, the Americans landed at the other end of North Africa. The local French authorities played a double game, though with extreme ineptitude, and the Americans did not reach Tunisia until Christmas. But it was a sign for Rommel that North Africa was over. He wrote, "I haven't much hope left. At night I lie with my eyes wide open, unable to sleep, for the load that is on my shoulders. In the daytime I'm dead tired."

He flew off to Rastenburg to see Hitler on 26 November and begged him to withdraw from a hopeless position. Hitler, in the throes of the Stalingrad imbroglio, would not see sense. He berated Rommel: "How dare you leave your theater of command without my permission?" and went on to tell Rommel that he would under no circumstances authorize a withdrawal from North Africa. "You are suggesting exactly the same as my generals last winter. I refused to allow it and events proved me right. There are sound political reasons why we must retain a bridgehead in North Africa. If we do not, there will be the most serious trouble in Italy." Rommel was, finally, dismissed, and reinforcements were sent to Tunisia. Army Group Africa came into existence under Arnim, with orders to hold out. Hitler stepped up the German element to 75,000 men with 280 of the new Panther series of tanks.

This decision did not have a happy outcome. Although the Anglo-Americans were extremely dilatory, they did proceed methodically enough, with safe supply lines and a large superiority. Arnim managed to inflict a humiliating reverse on the Americans in western Tunisia (at the Kasserine Pass) in February, but Montgomery's careful assemblage of force for a straightforward Montgomery-style battle of inescapable attrition wore the Germans down. By 7 April, the two Allied forces met up, and deployed 250,000 men (with 250,000 in the supply lines) to 120,000 Axis forces. In April, Axis supply vessels were sunk at such a rate that, even without any offensive action by the Allies, Arnim confessed he would have had to give in. In mid-May, this force surrendered, a loss to the Axis of 240,000 men. Hitler justified his strange reinforcement of this African corps with reference to the Italian situation: he claimed that "we managed to postpone the invasion of southern Europe by over half a year, and Italy has stayed in the Axis." But the cost had been much too high, for Italy was then wide open to invasion, and the numbers of men wasted in Tunisia might have altered the situation there out of all recognition.

As it was, Hitler was able to meet the Allied invasion of Italy almost without serious disruption of the war elsewhere. Many of the German generals were then quite defeatist. But experience of the Allied invasion of Italy, curiously, caused them to recover their will to win. On 10 July, the Allies landed in Sicily. No doubt, had they behaved with any imagination and dash, they could have cut off substantial German forces and enabled the Italians to escape from the German alliance more easily. As it was, an exceedingly slow, methodical progress was made along the circumference of Sicily; Kesselring, the German commander, evacuated his four divisions, forty-seven tanks, and seventeen thousand tons of supplies without any problem, even though clever ruses by the Allies had led, initially, to a disruption of German reserves all over southern Europe.

The Allied landing in Sicily was a signal to the Italian Opposition. Mussolini's position had been growing weaker with every defeat. He, unlike Hitler, had never eliminated such potential centers of opposition as the monarchy; also, unlike Hitler, he had allowed a Grand Council of the Fascist Party to remain in existence and here, theoretically, he could be outvoted. The dissident Fascists came together with the monarchy and some of the generals. Mussolini was defeated on a technicality, and, on 25 July, was declared deposed. Marshal Badoglio formed a new government. He pretended to adhere to the German alliance, but he interned Mussolini in a hotel in the mountains, and he undertook secret negotiations with the western powers. But he was very slow, and it was not until 8 September that he was ready to split with the Germans. By that time, the Germans were ready for him.

Divisions were sent south, to hold a very strong position in the mountains. Two divisions near Rome throttled the Italian revolt. Hitler sent his daredevil SS chieftain, Otto Skorzeny, to kidnap Mussolini, by glider, from his mountain retreat, and the hotel guards were startled out of their wits for a sufficient length of time for Mussolini to escape. Hitler installed him as puppet ruler of a Fascist republic in northern and central Italy. The German Tenth Army, under Vietinghoff, threw a cordon across the mountains of southern Italy. By contrast, the Allies were very slow indeed. Montgomery made an enormous bombardment of the extreme southern tip of the Italian peninsula, and then landed from Sicily. He found no resistance at all — the sledgehammer had not been used against even a nut. Then it took three weeks for the Allies to reach Naples, helped by another amphibious affair at Salerno. With winter, they stuck, with six German divisions holding fifteen double-strength Anglo-American ones. So it remained until the late spring of 1944.

This, and events elsewhere, caused some revival of German confidence. In June, Hitler had told Rommel in the Berghof that "he too was aware that there was very little chance of winning the war; but the West would never make peace with him, at least not while the present leaders were in charge, and now the West could have its war." Yet, whenever there was any question of making a peace with Russia, Hitler was strangely adamant. From time to time, there were indications that Stalin might like to exchange views. In September 1943, Dekanozov, who had been envoy in Berlin, turned up in Stockholm; conversations with intermediaries were held. Ribbentrop urged Hitler to explore the matter; there were indications, for instance, that Stalin might come to terms provided he obtained a free hand in Turkey. Hitler would not have this. "You know, Ribbentrop, if I made an agreement with Russia today, I'd still break it tomorrow — I just can't help it." Goebbels later submitted a forty-page memorandum on peace with Russia, and heard no more about it. Hitler hoped that the coalition against him would break up by itself; it was, after all, a very strange political animal. He assumed that a show of strength on Germany's part would hasten its disintegration.

Oddly enough, the German people at this time responded with resolution. Civilian morale remained very high. There is a great mystery here. Of course, the growing police state had something to do with it, especially in a country like Germany, many of whose inhabitants felt ill at ease if there were no tyrannical police around. Even in 1945, when the Americans had taken a village in Baden and the Gestapo had fled up the nearest mountain, inhabitants of the village would still solemnly go up the mountain to inform the Gestapo about their neighbors' defeatism. High morale partly reflected the activities of Goebbels's propaganda machine: just after Stalingrad, in February 1943, he delivered an immense speech demanding total war that brought a huge audience to frenzied enthusiasm.

There was also immense faith in Hitler himself, a factor that defies analysis. After Stalingrad Hitler himself became more and more withdrawn. He traveled through Germany with the carriage blinds drawn. He brooded more and more; he became, as Joachim Fest says, "dehumanized" and relapsed into "lachrymose misanthropy." He made only two major speeches after Stalingrad. And yet he retained a magical hold over most Germans. His reputation as miracle worker still carried people along in hope; there were dreams of secret weapons. His health, by spring 1943, was not good, and it seems to have been further undermined by the odd tonics that his doctor, Morell, prescribed. He had aged, and he needed spectacles, or a special typewriter with very large letters. Yet, as Rommel said, "What faith and power he radiates." In 1943, some religious-minded Germans began to organize resistance. But they were terribly isolated, and that isolation unnerved them so much that their resistance seldom went beyond talk. Quite ordinary security precautions defeated them.

One reason for the Germans' morale was paradoxical — British bombing. In the first six months of 1943, great raids were launched on the cities of the Ruhr, Hamburg, and Berlin. The most spectacular of these, the "Dam-busters" of 16 May broke reservoirs in the Ruhr and flooded whole districts. Ninety percent of Wupperthal was destroyed. Enormous air-raid towers were put up in the German cities; but the Allies discovered that their huge bombs, twelve-thousand-pound "earthquake" and twenty-two-thousand-pound "grand slam," could, if dropped around these constructions rather than on top of them, bring about "implosion." These bombing raids, though they smashed German homes into the strange moonscapes that only photographs can describe adequately, also provided the Germans with an obvious and very hated enemy. The war had not been popular in Germany in 1939. It became popular, in the sense of a universal, gripping will-to-win, in 1942 and 1943. Hitler symbolized this, as Churchill had done in Great Britain. The stumbling and aging figure, with his fanatical outbursts, dominated his people at this time. When, in February 1943, he left his East Prussian headquarters for a visit to Vinnitsa, an aide recorded that "it was strange, the hush that suddenly descended on the whole compound. It was as if the main dynamo had stopped. The puppet master, who held all the strings, had suddenly let them fall." This would have been applicable to Germany as a whole. Even the men of the German resistance shared his national aims; they differed only in the tactics they would use to gain them. There were, of course, alarms for morale at the time of Stalingrad. But when, in February 1942, Hitler told his Gauleiters, "If the German people fails, then it does not deserve our fighting for its future, we can just write it off," he had a sympathetic hearing.

The resolution was reflected in the war economy. In many occupied places, passive resistance and incompetent management were, of course, such that the Germans got very little out of them. In others, odd things happened. For whatever reason, production both in Belgium and in the Protectorate of Bohemia and Moravia rose — perhaps because of an administration that was (despite the many legends) comparatively mild and perhaps because there was no lack of enthusiastic collaborators in either place. Inside Germany, the Todt-Speer reforms of the winter of 1941–1942 brought about a considerable change. At that time, state interference was intelligent, the overlapping of army and ministerial agencies was curtailed, and the industrialists were associated in a sensible way, in committees and subcommittees. They too seemed, under the impact of bombing, to have responded well. There were still some terrible misjudgments on the part of the *Luftwaffe* organizers, and some prototypes continued to go badly wrong, dragging others down with them. But generally production rose from 11,800 in 1941 to 15,400 in 1942 and 24,800 in 1943 (in 1944: 40,000), as compared with Soviet figures, in the same period, of 15,700, 25,400, 35,000, and 40,300, or British figures of 20,100, 23,700, 26,500, and, again, 26,500. Since 1,500 planes had to be replaced monthly, German production was allowing expansion of the *Luftwaffe*. Only its absorption on the Russian front enabled the British bombing raids to penetrate German airspace so often. The reason for production improvement was quite simple: there was a great deal of room for improvement. The stress of bombing prompted the improvement to occur. Manufacturers suddenly discovered that they could make do with much less aluminum, for they could use wood instead. In 1941, 200,000 tons of aluminum had made 11,700 aircraft with a combined weight of 64,000,000 pounds. In 1942, 185,000 tons made 15,400 aircraft weighing 92,000,000 pounds; in 1944, 270,000 tons made 39,000 aircraft of 100,000,000 pounds. In the old days, there had been no standardization of parts, although a single ton of aircraft would have 32,000 different parts. Even bolts and screws were not standardized; the Junkers 88, for instance, had 4,000 different ones. This was now reduced to 200.

Finally, the very drafting of skilled labor to the front, as proper conscription was arranged, had a beneficial effect upon industry. It was now compelled to rely on semiskilled or even unskilled workers, many of them foreigners, and many of these, women. They could not form teams to build single aircraft. They were organized therefore according to specialty, on an assembly line, and the machine tools were rationalized. Thus, although at the Messerschmitt factory at Kempten only 23 percent of the labor force was skilled, and only 44 percent German, production had risen, by the end of 1942, by 42 percent. In the production of tanks it was the same: five hundred per month produced in 1942, and two thousand per month in 1943. In the summer of 1943 the *Wehrmacht* had 4.3 million men under arms, of which 3.3 million were on the Russian front. It was small surprise that confidence was regained after Stalingrad.

So far, the Russians' greatest virtue had been their resilience in defense. Their capacity for mobile offensive action had yet to be tested on a large scale; the spring of 1943 proved that it was still not great enough. In January, while the German evacuation from the Caucasus and the battle for Stalingrad were going on, the Russians had been able to probe the long flank of Army Group South in several places, dispelling satellite divisions and moving some way into the German rear, on the Donets. But the supply lines were too long and in winter conditions they could not sustain such an ambitious maneuver. In any case, many Russian commanders still had much to learn. The Soviet submarine force, for instance, was the largest in the world, but it sank, in 1942 and 1943 together, only one hundred ships in the Baltic. An amphibious landing was tried in February 1943 against the German position on the Black Sea coast, but it only showed how very sensible it was of the western powers to attempt such operations only with great prudence. Here, the Soviet tanks landed too far out, and their exhausts were swamped. The navy, acting according to plan, steamed off regardless of the situation and failed to use their naval guns. There was a massacre on the beaches, although a feint attack further along the coast was rather more successful. Similarly, the Soviet paratroops were thoroughly clumsy at this time.

The Red army could do quite well in February because the Germans had not had time to reorganize, but they were frustrated by Hitler's determination to hold on to his foothold in Asia — the Taman peninsula, just opposite the eastern side of the Crimea. Ruoff's Seventeenth Army and the two Panzer armies were kept for the defense of this position. Manstein, however, had taken charge of the entire area's defense; and he proved to be a first-class professional. He could appreciate the weaknesses of the Russian position and also see how they might be exploited, provided he were allowed to retire to a good line and use the troops he thus gained from shortening the line to form reserves. Hitler allowed this to be done. Rostov was lost in mid-February, and a new line was stabilized on the Mius, to the west. A Panzer army was sent to the northwest, where Kharkov already had fallen, and two Panzer corps, one of them a fresh SS one, were brought in from the west. At the same time, Hitler allowed evacuation of the salients held, at cost, by Army Groups Center and North. The Rzhev salient was abandoned in "Operation Buffalo" in March — an operation that was difficult because it meant leaving prepared positions to cross open ground with the enemy on three sides. In this operation, nothing of significance was lost. New reserves were formed.

The Russians, in mid-February, came south impetuously, hoping that they would cut off the Germans in a huge pocket on the Black Sea. But they had already lost heavily, and they were not well supplied. Manstein allowed them to probe forward, and he counterattacked. One Soviet army had its flank seized by a Panzer group; its discomfiture was exploited to attack the flank of the neighboring Soviet army, and intervention by fresh SS Panzer troops under Hausser completed the defeat. The Russians retired back over the Donets, losing Kharkov all over again, with twenty-three thousand dead and over six hundred tanks lost. Then the line stabilized, more or less where it had been at the start of "Blue" in June 1942. The only enduring monument to the Soviet advance was a large salient on the flanks of Center and South where the Russians had taken the city of Kursk.

Spring mud brought the front to a halt in March and both sides built up their resources. Hitler decided to try a new attack as soon as the ground became firm, and his new tanks, the Panthers and Tigers (Mark V and Mark VI), were ready. The Kursk salient was an obvious target, as the Izyum one had been a year before. Hitler's allies badly needed reassurance; the Finns had virtually suspended operations against the Red army, while the news from both Italy and Romania was not encouraging. The new attack, "Citadel," was meant to be "a beacon to the world." Hitler had qualms; he confessed to Goering, "Whenever I think about it, my stomach turns." But Zeitzler, Manstein, and Kluge, all of whom Hitler trusted, were in favor of the offensive. A very large force was assembled. At this time, the Germans had 279 divisions and 4,570 tanks or assault guns, of which 187 and 3,200, respectively, were in the east (apart from allied troops). The army would never again be as strong as this, and the generals wished to try for such an obviously good target as the Kursk salient.

The trouble was that their intentions were well known. It needed no genius to see that Kursk was a good place for attack. In any case, the British had broken the most secret German code, and informed the Russians by a route that even the Russians would trust. German preparations, and still more the lengthy delays in starting, allowed Russian commanders ample time for defense. They too built up a large force, so that, in the end, there were on each side about a million men, twenty-five hundred tanks, and twenty-five hundred aircraft. The Russians constructed six defensive positions, with five thousand mines sown per square mile, stretching over forty miles. The only accident favoring the Germans occurred when a Soviet bomber force that set out to bomb Kharkov airfield was itself surprised in the air. The great battle started on 4 July, and at once became an affair of attrition. German determination resulted in some penetration of the Soviet defenses, but by now the Russian tank commanders were wise to German tricks, and the Russian air force, properly equipped with dive bombers ("Shturmoviki") knocked out German tanks. On the southern side there was a gigantic tank battle, in which nine hundred tanks on each side maneuvered. The Germans did not break through; and by 11 July the affair was collapsing, even if Manstein doggedly went on reporting successes.

This week of action knocked out some twenty-five hundred German tanks, and cost such numbers of troops that the eastern front was then, generally, one-third lower than its establishment in numbers. The Russians, by contrast, had three men for every two Germans, and the proportion never declined thereafter. They exploited it immediately. On the northern side of the Kursk salient was a German salient, based on Oryol. It was attacked just as "Citadel" was ending, and fell by 22 July. Now, the German line was threatened everywhere south of Oryol. It stretched far out to the southeast, along the Donets, and then toward the Sea of Azov and the Taman peninsula. If the Russians broke through in the Kharkov area, then there would be a Black Sea "pocket" vast in size. On the other hand, Hitler's retreating would mean losing the Donets industrial area, with its many valuable minerals. Besides, any retreat would perhaps provoke Romania to leave the war. Hitler determined that there should be no retreats, or, if they had to happen, that they must be dogged. He wished to keep the foothold in Asia, where he constructed a position known as "Goth's Head" connected by a great bridge to Kerch, the easternmost point of the Crimea. If this position had to be evacuated, he wanted at least to protect the industrial region by holding the line of the Dniepr, one of the great Russian rivers, which flowed from Kiev toward the southeast, and then east, in a great bend toward the Black Sea, past the hydroelectric works at Zaporozhe. That bend would have to be held, otherwise all of the south-Russian industrial area would be lost, the Crimea would be cut off, and Hitler's hopes of impressing his allies would be ruined.

The Russians exploited one weakness after another, and summer conditions made their mobility much greater. They had quantities of American jeeps, and their recapture of Voronezh allowed them also to use their railways again. The Germans had lost very heavily at Kursk, so that there were, by September, three Russian fighters to one German — a ratio improved because, for some reason, the Russians always had a larger number of combatants per division than any other nation. In a British or a German division, half of the personnel would be engaged in supply or maintenance. In an American division, the number rose to three-quarters. In a Russian division it was one-quarter. Now, the Russians first attacked Kluge's central positions, driving him, by 31 August, to Smolensk. Early in August, they mounted a powerful attack on Kharkov, the southern edges of the Kursk salient. This too succeeded, and Kharkov was evacuated on 23 August. An attack further south, on the Sea of Azov, was threatened, and Manstein needed twelve divisions to cover the Kharkov area; he could have them only if he withdrew from the exposed positions east of the Dniepr bend. He did so on 4 September, the "Goth's Head" being evacuated by 25 September. On 21 September, the Russians had reached the Dniepr bend.

Hitler's options were closing one by one. He had to maintain troops in areas that were very unlikely to be attacked, so as to keep allies in the war. Thus, Army Group North and the forces in Finland were actually superior in number to the Russians but could do nothing because the Finns would not attack; and in the Crimea there were twenty-one divisions, also ineffective, kept there to impress the Romanians and the Turks. Yet the central part of the front was starved of troops: there was one division for twenty kilometers, whereas the Russians would attack with one division on three kilometers. There were no fixed positions of any seriousness, because there had been disagreements as to who was responsible for constructing them; the only good lateral railway from north to south was now menaced, in the Kiev area, and the reserves to defend it had had to go elsewhere. Hitler's insistence on no retreats was not, in the circumstances, at all helpful. Hitler himself saw this. His last visit to the eastern front in Russia occurred on 8 September, when he flew to Manstein's headquarters at Zaporozhe. When his aircraft lifted off, Russian tanks were only a quarter of a mile away. He left Manstein in charge and the results were as good as could be expected. A fighting retreat cost the Germans only ninety-eight thousand prisoners in the four months from Kursk to the end of the autumn, and half of these were wounded. Heavy antitank guns were maneuvered away with much efficiency. But it was no way to win a war.

The Russians continued with their effective methods. In early September, they switched their effort to the halfway point between Kiev and Zaporozhe, around Poltava, and broke through there. Then they concentrated on the southern side, and dislodged the Germans from Zaporozhe, causing a retreat to the eastern approaches to the Crimea. Early in November, with German reserves going south to counter this, they attacked on the other flank, and took Kiev on 6 November. They went rather rashly ahead after this, took Zhitomir, and then lost it again. Then there was a brief pause.

The curious thing was that, despite propaganda promoted by each side for different reasons, the German defeats were not brought about by the material strength of the Russians. On the contrary, the material position was less obviously in Stalin's favor than it had been at the time of "Barbarossa." Where the Russians gained was, first, through the pinning of so many German divisions to subsidiary fronts like the Crimea and Finland and, second, through their own vastly improved cooperation and mobility. One German general, Manteuffel, commented, "The advance of a Russian army is something that westerners cannot imagine. Behind the tank spearheads rolls a vast horde, largely on horseback. The horses eat the straw from the thatched roofs, and get very little else. The soldier carries a sack on his back, filled with dry crusts and raw vegetables collected, on the march, from fields and villages." Improvisation and ruthlessness coincided bizarrely in the Red army. To clear mine fields, Zhukov would send in punishment battalions. To carry heavy shell over slushy ground, he would use endless peasant women, their feet wrapped in cloth, each carrying a shell on her back. Bridges could be improvised in no time. Russian generals were, on average, twenty years younger than German ones. It was Hitler's system that was growing arthritic, in spite of the industrial effort that was going ahead.

From December to spring 1944, the Russian offensive in the south rolled on. No one had expected this. But the new Red army could manage a winter offensive and the German army could not. Hitler's strategy was, as before, concerned with the industries of the Dniepr bend, and thus he forfeited the flexibility he needed. On 24 December, Hoth's Panzer army was attacked west of Kiev; then, early in 1944, Army Group North was attacked at Leningrad, and it fell back fifty miles to Pskov and Narva. Kluge, at Army Group Center, would not give reserves to hold North, because he himself was being attacked on the upper Dniepr and so, by March, North retired to the eastern borders of the Baltic republics. Leningrad had at last been freed, after nearly a million of its people had been starved to death. In the south, Manstein was forced to send twelve divisions to cover the December breakthrough west of Kiev. His eastern flank became weak, and, on 5 January, Koniev attacked his central front south of Poltava. There was near disaster. Nine divisions, including the SS Viking division recruited in Scandinavia, were cut off early in February at the twin pockets of Korsun and Cherkassy. It needed all of the ingenuity that the Germans could command to save even thirty thousand of the hundred thousand men involved, and even then without their heavy equipment. This breakthrough spelled the end for the troops to the east. They retired in February from the Krivoy Rog and retreated toward Odessa. The Crimean forces were cut off. Odessa itself became a "pocket" as the German retreat went on to Romanian territory; it fell on 10 April. On Manstein's northern wing, then well to the west of Kiev, there was a further German reverse at Kameniec-Podolski; by 1 April the Russians had reached the Carpathians and the river Prut.

The last act of this period came in the Crimea. Hitler had forbidden its evacuation. He was worried that if the Russians took it, they would threaten Hitler's Balkan allies too effectively. Three hundred thousand men were penned in, although their general, Jaenecke, wished to retire. The men had been unaccustomed to hard work, for they had spent some months in the sun, drinking the Crimean wines. The onslaught of Red army men caused a panic, and, on 13 May, Sevastopol itself collapsed. The Germans, all save thirty thousand, were evacuated just in time, but the poor Romanians, of whom there were twenty-seven divisions, were captured. Now, the eastern front ran roughly along the old Soviet border. It came to a halt as the Russians gathered their strength for a new attack. It was to be combined with an invasion from the west.

13

Disintegration

HITLER HAD NOW PASSED into a world of fantasy, into which there were occasional flashes of the old intuitive powers. "My task," he told the generals in August 1944, "especially since 1941, has been never to lose my nerve, but always to find some way out if ever there is a crisis. For five years I have cut myself off from the world, and I live only for the fight." He still had his "will of iron" and he could still be, in one of his favorite phrases, "ice-cold," particularly when it came to the millions of deaths around him. He could even, still, inspire faltering generals. But his physical and nervous condition degenerated. Since Stalingrad, he had not been the same; as he said, "I have to relax and speak about something else. Otherwise I keep seeing the staff maps in the dark, and my brain goes grinding on and on. It takes me hours to get to sleep. If I put out the light, I can sketch exactly where every division was at Stalingrad. It goes on for hours till I get to sleep at five or six."

He had to change his strategy and take the West into account. It was true that the Allies' invasion of Italy had not been a success. They had been held at Monte Cassino in the winter of 1943–1944, had tried to outflank the line by an amphibious operation at Anzio in January, and had been held there too. They had managed to break through, after an enormous bombardment, as soon as the weather improved, but they had only inched their way forward to north of Rome by mid-June. But, now, they threatened to invade France. Great preparations had been going on in the south of England, and invasion could be expected at any stage from spring onward. Hitler's only possible strategy was to withdraw forces from the East, hope that the Allies would land in disorder, and try to defeat them. As British Intelligence put it, "several Stalingrads in the hope of one Dunkirk."

The morale of the German people remained astonishingly high. But there were several highly placed Germans who had also looked at the lessons of 1918, and who felt that it was time for a separate peace. These men were diplomats, army officers, and aristocrats, bound together by strong religious convictions and patriotism. They could talk to each other unguardedly because they were related, or belonged to much the same small social set. They would have liked to set Hitler aside without bloodshed, and some of them even imagined that they could do so by appealing to Heinrich Himmler, some of whose subordinates were, indeed, involved in the plotting. By 1943, however, it became clear that the only way to deal with Hitler was by assassination. The army officers tried, several times, to kill him, but something always went wrong. Still, by 1944, a military plot had come into existence by which the army could seize power. If the code name "Valkyrie" were issued by the headquarters of the reserve army in Berlin, troops would march to the government quarters, take over from the SS, and arrest the Nazi leaders, both in Germany and in occupied Europe. The plan was conceived, ostensibly, to cover an internal emergency. Two retired generals, Witzleben and Beck, would form a government, the head of which would be Carl Goerdeler, a member of the right-wing opposition.

The trouble was that these men had no contact within the Nazi Party leadership. When Mussolini was overthrown, it was as the outcome of Mussolini's own methods of ruling: he had left the monarchy in existence, had not kept the Church under control, and had been too lazy and inefficient, in the end, to make sure of a substantial section of his own party. In July 1943, all of these factions turned against him. Hitler, by contrast, knew how to divide and rule. There was no body at all — except, quite theoretically, the Reichstag until 1942 — where Hitler might be outvoted. He had promoted one Nazi after another and encouraged the resulting rivalries. Goering, Ribbentrop, Himmler, Goebbels, and Bormann fought for Hitler's ear, and when Albert Speer rose to a position of prominence in the war economy, he too struggled for power. These men distrusted, and in some cases hated, each other. They could never have joined forces for a plot, or indeed for anything else. Even when they were imprisoned for years on end in Spandau after the war, they would expend great energy on ignoring each other in the yard.

There were voices within the SS that urged Himmler to overthrow

Hitler and come to terms with one or another of the enemy powers. Himmler, after all, had a large and seemingly homogeneous and respectable force to back him; he and his lieutenants thought very highly of their own respectability; even men like Arthur Nebe, who had commanded one of the anti-Semitic detachments in Russia and who now ran part of the Gestapo, favored the officers' plot. Himmler was approached in 1942 and again in 1943. He sometimes seemed to respond favorably to the various hints. But he always drew back. Himmler was a man who, when he was telephoned by Hitler, would stand to attention and click his heels. Hitler knew his weakness: the grotesque respect for authority that distinguished so many Germans. Besides, were there not secret weapons? In any case, Himmler also had been bought. He was too slow-witted to embezzle funds and he prided himself on his incorruptibility. When he tired of his wife, he took up with a secretary and borrowed money from the Party chest to set her up in a villa near Bormann's wife in Berlin. This poor women probably had something to answer for in Himmler's failure to revolt. He probably knew that the plot was going on. But he did not join it, and when it went wrong, he was the plotters' worst enemy.

In the early months of 1944, the Gestapo began to penetrate the plotters' affairs. One group of opposition chiefs clustered around Admiral Canaris in military intelligence, but some were arrested in 1943. Another group met at the Silesian estate of Count Henry Moltke, whose mother was an Englishwoman. They too were penetrated. Finally, the month of June 1944 brought a great military crisis on both fronts, and the plotters decided to act.

The man designated to kill Hitler was a staff colonel, Count von Stauffenberg. Stauffenberg had been badly wounded in the war, and he obtained a place on the staff of the reserve army, which entitled him to attend Hitler's conferences. He made his contacts with sympathetic generals in the West, and took two bombs to these conferences. Two attempts failed from lack of opportunity, but a third came on 20 July, when Stauffenberg was due to attend a conference in the East Prussian headquarters. Stauffenberg was surprised in the lavatory when arming the second of his bombs, which he did not bother, in the end, to use. The other, armed, he placed in his brief case. It had a short time fuse, and Stauffenberg pushed the briefcase near to where Hitler was standing. He then made an excuse to leave, and went off by car to the airfield. As he left, there was a great explosion. Stauffenberg assumed that Hitler had been killed, with most of the inmates of the conference room, and he flew back to Berlin to organize the putsch.

Things went wrong from the start. There was no car for Stauffenberg to get to army headquarters. The plotters who gathered there were hesitant and divided. They had hoped to rely on General Fromm, Commander of The Reserve Army, but he played safe. Witzleben and Beck were testy, nonplussed. Finally, without waiting for Stauffenberg to arrive, the signal "Valkyrie" was given. What followed merely showed the isolation of these conspirators. In occupied Europe, military authorities received an order to arrest the SS leaders. In few cases did they do so. They were obviously mystified by the order. In Paris, Heinrich von Stülpnagel, who was involved in the plot, merely confined the SS and Gestapo chiefs in their hotel and drank champagne with them. In Berlin, soldiers marched to various key points, especially the government quarters. The soldiers there were led by a dedicated Nazi, Remer. When told to arrest Goebbels, he had very strong doubts. He explained these to Goebbels. Goebbels had a private line to Hitler, which the plotters had not been able to break. At six o'clock in the evening, Hitler came on the line. The attempt to kill him had failed. Whether a window had been opened in the conference hut (which would lessen the blast of the explosion), whether someone had pushed the briefcase further away from Hitler, or whether the heavy table helped shield the blast, the bomb had not done its work. Hitler's clothing had been badly torn by the blast, he had lost his hearing in one ear, and he never recovered his sense of balance. Some people in the hut had been killed outright. But Hitler had survived, even though in a state of shock. For some time, no one had reacted, thinking that the bomb must have been planted by Russians. It was only after details of Stauffenberg's journey back to Berlin became known that an army plot was sensed; and then, too, the breach in signals became explicable. Fellgiebel, a very courageous man who had charge of these signals, was arrested.

The rest was easy enough. Remer disobeyed the plotters' orders; instead, SS men and soldiers moved on the army headquarters to arrest the plotters. There was a brief, sad affair in which Beck tried several times, with a shaking hand, to shoot himself. Fromm had Stauffenberg and others shot in the courtyard, though this did not save him, in the end, from execution. Several other plotters killed themselves; they included highly placed generals such as Kluge and Stülpnagel in France. Then followed a Gestapo commission of investigation. Himmler sanctioned tortures of all kinds. He arrested even children who belonged to the conspirators' families — "you can read about this old Teutonic custom in the sagas," he told the Gauleiters. The officers were first expelled from the army and were then put before a "People's Court" where, unshaven, deprived of ties and suspenders, they behaved with extraordinary dignity. They then were executed — as Hitler said, "I want them strung up like slaughtered meat." A film was made by Goebbels for Hitler's edification as the men were strangled, slowly, with piano wire, suspended from meat hooks in Plötzensee prison. Gestapo investigation into the plot went on and on; and even in the last days of Berlin, the following April, executions were still going ahead.

From then on Hitler treated all of his generals as potential traitors. When he met them, he would be flanked by SS guards. Even Guderian and Zeitzler had their briefcases searched whenever they saw Hitler; no general dared to suggest retreat for fear he would become suspect. No one was safe from the last, mad antics of the SS. Though itself quite strongly infiltrated by upper-class men, it accounted for the deaths of some of the greatest names in Prussian history — Count von Moltke, Yorck von Wartenburg, Schwerin von Schwanenfeld, Lehndorff, von der Schulenburg, and Trott zu Solz. It was an appalling retribution for the casual way in which men of this class had intrigued against the Weimar republic.

Hitler himself was very badly shaken. This was shown almost at once, in one of the scenes of grotesque inappropriateness in which the Third Reich was to specialize from then on. There always had been tension between the Nazis' gangster leanings and their appeals to painful correctness. That tension finally errupted. In the afternoon of 20 July, Mussolini was due to arrive. He did so, a sort of Goering-sized Don Quixote, pendulous-cheeked, talking his amazing German. Hitler met him, white and trembling, and explained the miracle of his survival. There was a tea party. Recrimination started. Ribbentrop and Doenitz ranted at the generals who ranted back. Mussolini's own military chief, Marshal Graziani, tried to gloss this over by inflicting on the two dictators a monologue about his experiences in Africa. Then Hitler, who had been sitting in self-absorbed silence, burst out. He ranted wildly, on and on for half an hour, about what he would do to the guilty men's families. Silence fell on the quarrelling company. Graziani again tried to pretend that nothing out of the ordinary was happening, and talked technicalities with an embarrassed Keitel. Meanwhile, white-clad footmen circulated with silver teapots. There was a telephone call from someone wanting orders. Hitler took it, and again ranted orders to shoot everyone and anyone. "I am beginning to doubt if the German people is worthy of my ideals," he said. Then everyone protested their loyalty. The sight of Ribbentrop, architect of this war, doing so was too much for Marshal Goering. He started a violent quarrel with Ribbentrop, and, as the hubbub rose, even menaced Ribbentrop with his marshal's baton. The voice of

Ribbentrop was heard above the noise, protesting, "I am after all the foreign minister, and my name is *von* Ribbentrop." Such was the atmosphere of Hitler's court until the last, mawkish scenes in April.

By now, the military situation had begun to disintegrate. The western powers had resolved, at the Teheran conference of November 1943, to give priority to the invasion of France. A very large force was assembled in the south of England, with extremely thorough preparations. The shortest route over the Channel would of course have been to Calais, but the British preferred to make for the beaches of Normandy, hoping that they could seize the ports of Cherbourg and Caen, since they would need suitable harbors to unload the immense quantities of material that a successful invasion would demand.

German preparations were not very efficient. There was much disagreement about use of the armor. Rommel, who had charge of the western defenses, wished to use the tanks to form a wall on the Channel, but the chief of the Panzer troops preferred to have the armor used as a mass, for a great counterattack. In the end, there was compromise: the armor was split up, but at a considerable distance from the coast. On top of this, the commanders guessed wrongly as to where the invasion would come, and they placed almost half of their troops at or near Calais. Hitler had guessed that Normandy would be the target, but he could not overrule everyone in the western High Command, and he let the generals place their troops as they wished. After all, he had done reasonably well in shaping up to the invasion. His new strategy was perhaps not original, but it made sense. He had had sixty divisions, and seventeen Panzer ones, sent to the West, and had run down his forces in Russia to two-fifths of the army's strength. These forces ought, he supposed, to be enough to counter the Allies' thirty-eight divisions, with their difficult supply lines over the Channel.

The invasion occurred on 6 June 1944, and coincided with resistance action in France. Allied air cover was overwhelming, so much so that German Panzer divisions hardly could move by day; the communications network had been disrupted to such an extent that, of one hundred trains needed to serve the front, the German Army Group B was lucky to receive thirty, and most of its movement was made by bicycle. Allied supplies moved to artificial harbors known as "Mulberries," an ingenious device that altogether astonished the Germans, who failed, for many weeks, to see the huge numbers of Allied soldiers and vehicles that were crossing successfully. Eighty-seven thousand men and 7,000 vehicles were landed on 6 June; by 18 June, the figures were 629,000 and 95,000, and by 29 July, 1,666,000 and 333,000.

On 6 June itself, and generally in the first days of the invasion, the German armor was too far off to intervene. Only one Panzer division could come in, and it took fourteen hours to do so. The Allies built up a strong enough bridgehead to protect their stores from German artillery. Even so, when the German armor came in, there followed bitter action. It took the British a month to capture Caen, and although the Americans, driving northwest, captured Cherbourg, it was in extremely battered condition. Up to 15 August, there was a hard and bitter battle of attrition, in which only the Americans, who had some leeway into Brittany, had any kind of capacity for maneuver. But this was the kind of battle in which Montgomery was a specialist. He could organize titanic bombardments from artillery and aircraft. Rommel gave Montgomery almost as good as he got, and up to 20 July the British had been penned in on their bridgeheads. But the Americans cut to the southwest, and when they had reached the flank of the Germans holding Montgomery, the German line broke. In the Falaise pocket were forty-five thousand prisoners, though Montgomery later believed that the German defeat should have been greater. By 23 July, the Germans had lost 110,000 of their million men, and these losses were not replaced. The Allies' losses, however, 117,000, were at once made up. Of 2,000 German tanks, only 120 had escaped to the Seine by 18 August. In the end, the Germans' retreat took them out of France altogether. Paris was freed on 24 August, by which time the Germans had lost 400,000 men and the Allies 240,000.

Rommel himself had been injured by Allied aircraft on 17 July and was replaced by Kluge and then Model. Before his accident, he telegraphed Hitler, "Our men are fighting heroically but the unequal struggle is nearing its end. I must ask you to draw the necessary conclusions — it is my duty as commander in chief to say this plainly." But Hitler was still adamant. He saw the western generals on 17 June near Soissons, and he spoke to them again at Berchtesgaden a fortnight later. On both occasions his message was simple: fight on. He had prepared a rocket bomb, the V1, that he thought would terrify the population of London; its successor, the V2, was even more terrifying. Besides, would not the enemy coalition fall apart? He told the generals plainly that the time was not ripe for "a political solution." They must fight on. He was proved right. The Allies' supply lines lengthened as they went on in France, and the invasion force became somewhat disordered. It reached the rivers — the Rhine, the Moselle, the Meuse — and captured Antwerp on 4 September. But that port was not put into working order for some time, and a British paratroop drop into Holland, at Arnhem, had failed by mid-September. Then, and for the next few months, the Allies could only grind forward against strong German positions. Perhaps the bold stroke through northwestern Germany that Montgomery advocated would have worked, and, as Liddell Hart believed, would have saved the western powers the half million casualties they incurred from then on in the liberation of Europe. But the Allies were too slow and, in this case, too divided.

On the eastern front, the Russians, too, failed to win a decisive victory, though they came very close to it. They began a fresh offensive on 22 June, on the front of Army Group Center, on the upper Dniepr. Hitler had run down the eastern forces, from 80 percent in June 1943 to 40 percent in June 1944, and of these, Army Group Center was the weakest, for it had lost troops to other groups. Its armor had been placed on its right flank, to fend off a Russian threat, in the spring, to Kovel. It is not too much to say that Hitler coldly sacrificed the men of this army group. He wanted time; sacrifice of the forty-five divisions here would give it to him. The commander, Busch, was an ardent Nazi. He was pushed by his subordinates to ask Hitler for permission to withdraw to a shorter line, with better possibilities of retreat, than the existing one, which was 150 miles longer than it need have been and the approaches of which ran along forest tracks that could be blocked by partisans. Hitler forbade any retreat and snubbed Busch for even asking: he was "frankly surprised that Busch was among those soldiers who looked round over their shoulders." He also told Busch to keep half of his troops in strongpoints like Vitebsk or Orsha, instead of remaining mobile. The forces in the strongpoints were even allowed to command the mobile troops outside. In other words, everything that could be done to wreck the situation was done. The only excuse was that Hitler would gain time to defeat the western powers.

The end of Army Group Center was yet another of the nightmares of the eastern front. Russian superiority was incalculable: one hundred thirty infantry divisions, thirty-five armored divisions, six thousand aircraft, and fifty-two hundred tanks to the Germans' weak forty-five divisions, forty aircraft, and two hundred tanks, most of them in the wrong tactical position. The result was a foregone conclusion, especially since Hitler ordered his forces to stay put until wiped out. By 3 July, the Russians had taken Minsk, and destroyed twenty-eight divisions. Three hundred fifty thousand Germans were taken prisoner and triumphally marched through Red Square as evidence of Stalin's power. There was a breach of 250 miles where Army Group Center had been, and the new strong Russian mechanized corps moved into it, covering 160 miles in ten days. By the end of July, the Red army was on the Vistula; it had also invaded the Baltic states and for a time severed the link, in Lithuania, between Army Group North and what remained of Center. North withdrew hastily toward Riga and restored the link only with difficulty. However, despite the uprising of Poles in Warsaw, the Red army waited for supplies and reserves for another large effort in the center and north. But it continued its offensive in the south.

In July, the Russians used their breakthrough in Center to occupy southern Poland, inflicting a sharp defeat on the Germans at Brody, and taking Lwów on 28 July. They continued into Romania. On 20 August, Rodion Yakovlevich Malinovski moved. He encountered, in Bessarabia, three hundred thousand Germans and eight thousand demoralized Romanians. The front was bisected by deep valleys; relations between the Germans and Romanians were poor. The front of Army Group South Ukraine, as South was then known, collapsed. Then came disaster. The young king of Romania had only been waiting for the favorable moment to stage his coup against Antonescu. With the help of guards and generals, he imprisoned Antonescu on 23 August and invited the Russians into his country. Two hundred thousand Germans were caught in this trap, and the Balkans lay open to the Red army.

By early September, Bulgaria had joined the Russian coalition, and the Germans were forced to evacuate Greece, southern Yugoslavia, and finally Belgrade as well in October. Then it was Hungary's turn. The ruler of Hungary tried to make an armistice with the Russians on 15 October. But his country was occupied by the Germans, who had their own contacts with Hungarian Nazis. The coup failed; the ruler was kidnapped by the ineffable Otto Skorzeny; and a pro-Nazi government, that of Ferenc Szálasi, was moved in. Hitler was determined to defend his oil, and he made a particular effort to defend the Hungarian wells of Nagykánizsa. By December, he had held the Russian attacks in central Hungary and northern Yugoslavia. This enabled Eichmann's henchmen to persecute hundreds of thousands of Hungarian Jews. The middle-European heartland had held out well enough against the Red tide: resistance had stiffened, and the Red army had outrun its supply line. The front ran through central Hungary, the eastern borders of Slovakia (which had also vainly rebelled in the late summer) and central Poland. In the north, the Germans had been pushed in October into an enclave of territory northwest of Riga. Fifty divisions, known as "Army Group Courland," held on there until the end of the war, supplied by sea. This line, like the line along the rivers in the west, had stabilized — much to everyone's surprise. To break it would require one last effort.

14

The Last Ditch

THE SEPTEMBER HALT had come as a surprise. But now the end was in sight, even if there were still not a few fanatical Nazis who believed in the *Führer*'s secret weapons and who contrived to believe that Hitler was merely allowing the enemy to penetrate Europe too far, so that he could launch a counteroffensive. By October, the western powers had found a way to prevent the Germans from launching any more attacks. They had invented a fighter, the Mustang, which could fly fifteen hundred miles and back and which could provide cover for day bombers. This meant that key industrial works, such as those producing synthetic fuel, could be hit in daylight. There were only five of these works, and they were duly put out of commission in October, when the great Krupp works also ceased production. Speer was still producing aircraft. But the aircraft could not go into the air for lack of oil, and the Allies bombed them to pieces on the ground. On the few occasions when the *Luftwaffe* took to the air, aircraft had to be towed onto the airfields by oxen. Hitler's inventors had created a rocket-propelled plane and, with the Me-262, they also had produced a jet fighter that, for a few days in March, achieved astonishing results. But fuel supplies were so low that these good aircraft were of no use. The tanks similarly were impeded.

Hitler's final effort at an offensive was launched on the western front in mid-December 1944. The Allies had settled down for the winter, rather shaken by the losses they had incurred in their nibbling at strong German positions along the rivers. They did not expect the Germans to find any more strength than they had. Nor, to be fair, did the German generals. They told Hitler that to attack would be folly, merely a way of throwing away the last chance of fighting a last-ditch resistance stiff enough for the Allies to want to come to terms. But Hitler insisted on his final offensive.

He chose the Ardennes yet again. Here, the Americans were weak; and a serious thrust might bring the attackers to Liège or perhaps even Antwerp. He summoned the generals to a conference at his western headquarters near Giessen in Hesse. The generals were driven around and around, in an effort to confuse them as to the direction their cars were taking. When they reached headquarters, they were searched; and at the conference itself, as Rundstedt remarked, after the war, "not one of us would have dared even to take out a handkerchief." These men were given Hitler's instructions, so precise that hardly a sentry could be moved from a door to a window without his permission. The attack was led off by two armored groups, one of them under Sepp Dietrich, commander of Hitler's bodyguard. For a time, it achieved some success. Then lack of fuel and Allied air control brought it to a stop. By early January, the Allies were counterattacking. Guderian, who had succeeded Zeitzler, wanted Hitler to retreat from the territory he had gained. He was told: "I have the horrors every time the word retreat is mentioned. I've heard that kind of thing for the past two years and the results have always been terrible." The Ardennes offensive had one serious effect only: it deprived the Germans of reserves with which they might have faced the Russians.

On 12 January, the Red army began to move again, on the Vistula. Curiously enough, Hitler did exactly the same to Army Group Center as he had done in the previous June. He stripped it of troops, partly for the sake of the relatively successful counteroffensive near Budapest and partly because he would not abandon his Baltic outpost. Since October, Army Group North had been isolated in Courland, to no effect at all, since the Finns made their peace with the Russians in September. But Hitler would not withdraw it. Army Group Center had seventy weak divisions to cover three hundred miles of front. Of the Panzer divisions, seven were in Hungary, two in Courland, four in East Prussia, and five in Brandenburg. Slovakia was also overgenerously covered. But Hitler dismissed tales of Russian strength in Poland: "It's the biggest pretense since Genghis Khan." He assumed the Russians, from their vast losses, must be using fifteen-year-old boys. In reality there was an enormous force: one hundred sixty-three divisions with sixty-four hundred tanks, five thousand aircraft, and two million men. Again, there was a disaster.

The Russians broke out over the Vistula at once, and within two weeks they were overrunning Poland, threatening Silesia, and invading East Prussia. Half a million Germans were lost, and the remainder were chased away.

By mid-February, forty divisions, or two hundred fifty thousand men, were confined in pockets along the Baltic at Königsberg-Samland, Heiligenbeil, and Danzig, quite apart from the divisions trapped in Courland. The Russians reached the Oder, and in the same period captured Budapest as well. Perhaps they could have captured Berlin had they gone on resolutely; indeed, the Russians argued among themselves, after the war, as to whether, had they been quicker in February, they might not have reached the Ruhr before the western powers did — a curious counterpart to the parallel allied debate as to whether the western powers could not have reached Berlin first. Instead, Stalin preferred to clear up the various German pockets: Danzig held out until the end of March, Königsberg until 9 April, and Courland to the very end. In the south, the Russians had their hands full with western Hungary, though they took Vienna in mid-April. Meanwhile, in the center, they were held by the resilient defense of the fortresses of Poznan and Breslau. It was not until mid-April that they were ready again to go over the Oder at Berlin.

The western front, too, was falling apart. Hitler had had to shift divisions from it, and in February and March the British made a methodical march into the Netherlands. On 6 March, the Americans had taken Cologne, and at the same time, to the south, daring improvisation gave them an intact Rhine bridge at Remagen. Omar Bradley himself crossed by boat and, with the sense of occasion on which he and Patton prided themselves, urinated into the Rhine. Montgomery, to the north, staged a methodical envelopment of the German army group defending the middle Rhine. By 16 April, 350,000 men were caught in the British grip. They surrendered, and their commander, Model, shot himself. Further south, the Americans simply walked forward to the river Elbe, where they met up with the Russians on 27 April. By then there was hardly any resistance at all in the West, and the number of prisoners, which made up a very small proportion of casualties in the East — where resistance was still fanatical — accounted for almost all of the casualties in the West.

The new Russian offensive on Berlin began, with two hundred divisions and a vast array of material against fifty divisions, on 16 April. And by 25 April, Berlin was encircled by three Russian army groups. It was defended by the remnants of an imposing force, which included the French SS division "Charlemagne," police brigades, and the Home

Guard consisting of old men and young boys that Goebbels had promoted. The Allies, and some Germans, supposed that there were intact
armies to the north, in Pomerania, and to the south, in Silesia. A "Bavarian Redoubt" was also in existence, and Munich had not yet been
captured. The last act of Hitler's life therefore occurred while illusions
prevailed.

Apart from a few Nazi fanatics and some of the SS, not many people
shared these illusions. Northern and eastern Germany were scenes of
pandemonium. As the Russians advanced, millions of Germans fled
before them — some by sea from Courland and East Prussia, some over
the ice, and others in an endless, terrified trudge. Through the millions
came Allied and Russian planes. While the cities of Germany were
smashed into rubble, their inhabitants crowded into cellars. Ex-collabo-
rationist foreign potentates, still ludicrously insisting on their dignity, got
in the way, and, through it all, moved hideous columns of prisoners from
the concentration camps, being evacuated as the Allied armies approached. In the evacuation from Ravensbrück, the wife of an SS officer
sat in a cart pulled by six female skeletons, making herself sick on
raisins. In Berlin, Gestapo squads still filed through the moonlike landscape, carrying out their deadly work with the automaton brutality of
the police mind at its dimmest. Several of the best men in Germany fell
victim in the very last days of the Reich. Smashed cities, inhabited by
starving wretches and led by bureaucrats still dimly mumbling the lit-
anies of their days of greatness, were a suitable monument to the end of
the SS empire.

In the midst of all of this rubble, Hitler went on hoping. Perhaps the
enemy coalition would fall apart; perhaps his armies would bring the
Russians to a halt. He had left East Prussia in November. Now he
retired to the Reich Chancellery in Berlin. The bombing was too much,
and that vast building began to suffer from it — windows were boarded
up, the garden was a mass of bomb craters, and a fine dust spread over
everything. Several of the other government buildings had been hit.
Hitler decided to retire to the bunker he had had constructed. For a time,
he surfaced for meals; then he gave that up, and simply lived in the
bunker.

The bunker had been built in the gardens of the Reich Chancellery. It
was reached by a flight of steps to a steel door guarded by two SS men,
through which visitors would go down another flight of steps to a corri-
dor in which there was a foot of water. The visitors would then totter
across duckboards, descend further steps, and enter a central hall that
acted as a mess room and a center for the twelve small rooms off it.

There was a curving stairway down to a further floor, where Hitler lived.
In his quarters were eighteen cubicles, separated by an entrance hall that
doubled as conference and waiting room. Beyond that there was an
emergency exit to the garden two hundred feet above. Hitler had a suite
of six small rooms for himself and Eva Braun and his dog; in the days of
disaster, he came to depend on their companionship. The bunker had a
twelve-foot thick cement ceiling with thirty feet of concrete above that.
Time, in this world, had no meaning, as the air-conditioning whined and
the staff went in and out. Hitler's military conferences would end at six
in the morning. He himself was a nervous wreck, stoop-shouldered, all
atremble. He quieted his nerves as best he could. In the Reich Chancellery were kept wooden models of the great Linz that was to be built.
Hitler would sometimes stumble across the rubble in the gardens to go
and inspect these models, with much gushing appreciation of the architects' designs. His appetite for cake, always considerable, became quite
ferocious. After conferences, his manservant would tuck his feet up on
the sofa, and Hitler would be passed the plate. In the old days, he would
have confined himself to three pieces. Now, he heaped his plate with it
every time, and always passed it back for more.

Discipline in the bunker began to slacken. Hitler had never been good
at exacting it from his intimates without a great effort. People, however,
no longer rose when Hitler entered a room, nor did they automatically
stop talking. Even so, his presence haunted the place. His staff and most
of his officers were still caught by the extraordinary spell of this man, and
they feared his tantrums. Even men who came to "tell the *Führer* the
facts" would simply be astounded. Front officers with high decorations,
who came to receive an honorific conversation with their leader and who
would hope to put in an oar or two for sanity, would listen dumbfounded
to his monologues (for, however brave they had been, he did the talking
on such occasions). Some even went away invigorated, ready to face the
next disaster. As for the generals, they were like mollusks caught in an
ice age.

As disaster followed upon disaster, some of the Nazi leaders began to
think at least of stirring a polyp toward the West. The limit of Himmler's power had been reached in February. Hitler gave him command of
an army group in the east, with the hope that Himmler would inspire
fanatical resistance, at least in SS divisions. The strain was too much for
Himmler, who knew nothing at all about war. He retired to a sana-
torium at Hohenlychen, living on a diet of strychnine, belladonna, and
hormone tonic. There, he was besieged with demands from subordinates
that he initiate peace discussions. Late in February and again in April,

he received a representative of the Swedish Red Cross, to consider the fate of the Scandinavian prisoners. He tried to ingratiate himself with the Swede with references likely to kindle the Swede's nordic feelings: did the Japanese alphabet not disclose affinities with the old Teutonic runes? He finally asked the Swede to use his good offices with the western powers to find out if they would consider negotiating with him; he wanted to know from the Swede, as "one man of the world to another, should I offer my hand to General Eisenhower when I meet him." There was a similar, extraordinary, meeting between Himmler and a representative of the world Jewish organization. Himmler suggested, "It is time that we Germans and you Jews buried the hatchet." Ribbentrop, who was in charge of what was left of foreign policy since the world had declared war on Germany, had similar ideas. But neither man dared to make the first move for fear of being denounced to Hitler by the other. Negotiations for a separate armistice on the Italian front did come to something, late in April, after the end of Mussolini; but even that was not an easy matter.

No glimmer of reality invaded the bunker. In mid-April, Hitler informed Ribbentrop that there must be no separate negotiations with the Russians: "We may fall in the fight against Bolshevism, but we will never negotiate with it." He played Wagner's *Götterdämmerung* on the gramophone and resolved, as he contemplated the dripping concrete walls and the lush hangings of his section of the bunker, that there should be a proper end to Valhalla. His last public appearance occurred on his birthday, 20 April, when he passed before a line of Hitler-Youth Home Guards. He then celebrated his birthday and told his followers that he meant to go down fighting in Berlin. He dismissed several of them, including Goering, who was sent off south with fourteen carloads of clothing and treasure from Karinhall, to organize the "Bavarian Redoubt."

There was still some hope left, and up to 22 April Hitler nourished ideas that someone would come to his rescue. But he was dealing in phantom armies and groups, the realities of which were a few shivering, weaponless boys or directionless policemen. By the evening, even Hitler had given up hope, as no news came through by radio of the relief offensive. His nerve broke. He stormed and raged, shouting that he was surrounded by liars and traitors. "It is all finished, National Socialism is dead and can never rise again." Bormann telephoned Goering to give him this news; and Goering went ahead to send a telegram to Hitler demanding authorization to enter peace discussions with the Allies. He made out, possibly with Bormann's encouragement, that he did not know whether Hitler was still alive and that, if he heard nothing within two days, he would act. Bormann, who no doubt had acted quite deliberately in this way so as to discredit Goering, showed Hitler the telegram. Hitler decided, in another storm of rage, to dismiss Goering. Word was sent south for him to be arrested and stripped of office. He was in fact put under house arrest, and he signed his resignation at SS insistence. His successor as head of the *Luftwaffe*, Greim, flew with what remained of the force's petrol to Berlin to receive instructions. He had to land on the great Nazi boulevard running through the center of Berlin, and his foot was smashed by a Russian shell. He was immobilized for a time in the bunker, until Hitler packed him off again with orders to deal with the "traitors."

The next of these proved to be Himmler. On 27 April, a neutral radio announced that negotiations had been going on between the SS and the Allies. This coincided with the news that the SS liaison officer in the bunker, Fegelein, had deserted. He had decided, and there was no link between his decision and Himmler's, that the time had come for good rats to leave. He took some foreign money and went to his flat in western Berlin. He was the first casualty of Himmler's negotiations. A grim SS guard picked its way through the Berlin rubble, with Russian shells whining overhead, and found Fegelein, reading cheap novels in his flat. He was brought back, and shot.

There remained a small knot of the faithful in the Chancellery. Goebbels and his family had moved in on 22 April; Bormann was there; Axmann of the Hitler Youth; Burgdorf of army personnel; assorted secretaries and servants. Hitler had now decided: he would kill himself. On 28 April, the Russians neared the Reichstag building, only a few hundred yards from the bunker. He had his political testament drawn up and copies made, and appointed Doenitz as his successor. Then he decided to marry Eva Braun. Just before midnight on 28 April, this bizarre ceremony took place. There happened to be a minor official in a nearby Home Guard unit who was competent to perform a civil ceremony. He was duly brought in. The rings were obtained from a Gestapo treasurer. Afterward, there was a wedding breakfast, with cut glass and silver, and eight guests.

The next day, 29 April, passed with agonizing slowness. Nerves were strained, and everyone was smoking — which in Hitler's entourage had always been forbidden. By six o'clock in the evening, the full desperation of the situation in Berlin was quite clear, and Hitler also heard, from the radio, that Mussolini had been hung upside down outside a garage in Milan. He determined to have his own corpse burned to avoid such indignity. Then, at midnight, he said good-bye to his staff and retired. He took his valet aside and instructed him on how the corpses should be burned. Then he and Eva Braun sat on a sofa. She bit into her poison capsule; Hitler put a bullet through his right temple. A spirit of frivolity entered the bunker: the junior staff put dance tunes on the gramophone. Berlin surrendered; and a week later, the Reich itself agreed to the unconditional surrender on which the Big Three had insisted.

Bibliographical Notes

THESE NOTES are primarily intended as a guide for further reading in the English language. They are highly selective, as space does not allow me to include the majority of my own sources, so that I have had to omit mention of some distinguished monographs. I have cited German-language material only where it is essential. A full bibliography of works on nazism may be found in Norman Rich, *Hitler's War Aims* (New York, 1973–74), and many of the books or articles that have appeared since then are cited in W. Carr, *Hitler: A Study in Personality and Politics* (London, 1978). The most comprehensive lives of Hitler are Joachim Fest, *Hitler: A Biography* (New York, 1970) and Alan Bullock: *Hitler: A Study in Tyranny* (Revised Edition, 1967).

Chapter 1

The most thorough investigation of Hitler's early years is W. Maser, *Adolf Hitler* (London, 1972). R. G. L. Waite, *Hitler, the Psychopathic God* (London, 1977) makes interesting, often well-founded speculations on Hitler's character. Recent German works include Albrecht Tyrell, *Vom "Trommler" zum "Führer"* (Munich, 1975) and W. Horn, *Führer-ideologie und Parteiorganisation in der NSDAP* (Düsseldorf, 1972). The most comprehensive account of the putsch is H. J. Gordon, *Hitler and the Beer Hall Putsch* (Princeton, 1972). The development of Hitler's ideology can be investigated through D. C. Watt's edition, *Hitler's "Mein Kampf"* (London, 1968), while the precise circumstances surrounding the work are revealed in W. Maser, Hitler's "Mein Kampf" (Munich, 1966). D. Orlow, *History of the Nazi Party* (2 Vols., London, 1972–3), digests a great deal of material.

Chapter 2

We are not well-served in English as regards the details of German politics in the last years of the Weimar, especially for the connections between finance and politics. Gordon Craig, *Germany: 1866–1945* (Oxford, 1978), provides an excellent survey and bibliography; but there is no substitute in English for K. D. Bracher, *Die Auflösung der Weimarer Republik* (Wiesbaden, 1963), or for H. Brüning, *Memoiren* (2 Vols., Stuttgart, 1970), blow-by-blow accounts of political maneuvering. Other German works on which I have relied very heavily, especially on economic matters, are the edition by Hans Mommsen et. al. (eds.), *Industrielles System und politische Entwicklung in der Weimarer Republik* (Düsseldorf, 1974); Dieter Gessner, *Agrardepression und Präsidialregierung in Deutschland 1930–1933* (Düsseldorf, 1977); Ludwig Preller, *Sozialpolitik in der Weimarer Republik* (new edition, Düsseldorf, 1977); D. Petzina, "Hauptprobleme der deutschen Wirtschaftspolitik" in *Vierteljahrshefte f. Zeitgeschichte*, 15 (1967); H. Köhler, "Arbeitsbeschaffung, Siedlung und Reparationen in der Schlussphase der Regierung Brüning" in *ibid.* 17 (1969); H. Köhler, "Sozialpolitik von Brüning bis Schleicher" in *ibid.* 21 (1973); W. Conze and H. Raupach (eds.), *Die Staats-und Wirtschaftskrise des Deutschen Reiches* (Stuttgart 1967); H. A. Turner, *Faschismus und Kapitalismus in Deutschland* (Göttingen, 1972); and H. Marcon: *Arbeitsbeschaffungspolitik der Reg. Papen Schleicher* (Frankfurt, 1974). In English, R. Manvell and H. Frankel, *The Hundred Days to Hitler* (London, 1974); A. J. Nichols and E. Matthias (eds.), *German Democracy and the Rise of Hitler*; D. Petzina, "Germany and the Depression" in *Journal of Contemporary History*, 4, 1969. W. S. Allen, *The Nazi Seizure of Power* (London, 1965), is a valuable local study.

Chapter 3

The political side of the new regime is well-covered in English; Joachim Fest surveys these years in detail. Other important works are: H. Höhne, *The Order of the Death's Head* (New York, 1970); David Irving, *The War Path* (London, 1978); Franz Neumann, *Behemoth* (New York, 1944); R. J. O'Neill, *The German Army and the Nazi Party* (London, 1964); F. Tobias, *The Reichstag Fire* (London, 1964), the findings of which have not, I believe, effectively been challenged, despite strong efforts; L. Snyder, *Encyclopaedia of the Third Reich* (New York, 1976).

Chapter 4

On the economic side, especially, it is only recently that historians have come to terms with a problem that, for many years, was not even posed by many of them. G. Stolper et. al., *The German Economy: 1870 to the Present*

(New York, 1967), and K. E. Poole, *German Financial Policies: 1932–1939* (New York, 1939), are thorough, if rather traditional, in approach. They have to be corrected by C. W. Guillebaud, *The Economic Recovery of Germany* (London, 1939), and B. H. Klein, *Germany's Economic Preparation for War* (new edition, London, 1967). The present-day state of debate in Germany can be judged from D. Petzina, *Die deutsche Wirtschaft in der Zwischenkriegszeit* (Wiesbaden, 1977), and H. L. Volkmann et. al. (eds.), *Wirtschaft und Rüstung am Vorabend des Zweiten Weltkrieges* (2 Vols., Düsseldorf, 1975). In English, the essential work is that done by A. S. Milward, *The German Economy at War* (London, 1964), and by R. J. Overy, "Cars, Roads, and Economic Recovery in Germany" in *Economic History Review*, 2nd ser., 28 (1975), R. J. Overy, "Transportation and Rearmament in the Third Reich" in *Historical Journal*, 16 (1973); R. J. Overy, "The German *Motorisierung* and Rearmament: a Reply" in *Economic History Review*, 32 (1979). In this last is given as comprehensive a list of figures for arms spending as we are likely to have. These figures mark an increase over those given by Klein, who seems to have underestimated construction spending on the *Westwall*. The new figures do not, however, restore the old picture of Hitler as a maniacal spender on weapons of war. Overy's Ph.D. thesis for Cambridge University is "The Luftwaffe in the German Economy" (1976). I have also benefited from the text of a lecture by A. S. Milward (May 1979) on "The Reichsmark Bloc and the International Economy." In this area, two recent works deserve mention: L. Neal, "The Economics and Finance of Bilateral Clearing Agreements" in *Economic History Review*, 2nd ser., 32 (1979), and P. Marguérat, *Le 3ᵉ Reich et le pétrole roumain* (Leiden, 1977). D. Petzina's *Autarkiepolitik im Dritten Reich* (Stuttgart, 1968) is an essential study of the Four Year Plan in operation.

On the political and social side, an excellent introduction to the question of Hitler's popularity is J. P. Stern, *Hitler, The Führer and The People* (London, 1972). D. Schoenbaum, *Hitler's Social Revolution* (London, 1967), and Richard Grunberger, *A Social History of the Third Reich* (London, 1975), should be read together with T. W. Mason, *Arbeiterklasse und Volksgemeinschaft* (Opladen, 1978). M. Broszat et. al., *Anatomy of the SS State* (London, 1968), and H. Deutsch, *Hitler and his Generals* (Minnesota, 1976), offer useful information; also U. D. Adam, *Judenpolitik im Dritten Reich* (Düsseldorf, 1973). On the personalities and "style" of the regime: Albert Speer's *Inside the Third Reich* (London, 1970) can be complemented by H. Giesler, *Ein Anderer Hitler* (Leoni am Starnbergersee, 1978), and J. Thiess, *Architekt der Weltherrschaft* (Düsseldorf, 1976). P. Bleuel, *Sex and Society in the Third Reich* (London, 1968), is a very revealing work.

Chapter 5

"Revision" of the Nuremberg version of the outbreak of war in 1939 began in book form with A. J. P. Taylor, *The Origins of the Second World War* (London, 1973 edition). In recent years, the confusion of Hitler's foreign affairs has been played up. S. Aster, *The Making of the Second World War*

(London, 1973), is a very thorough piece of work but should be read in context with K. Hildebrand, *The Foreign Policy of the Third Reich* (London, 1974), and the works on economic aspects cited above. Two useful recent German collections are M. Funke (ed.), *Hitler, Deutschland und die Mächte* (Düsseldorf, 1976), and H. L. Volkmann (ed.), *Kriegswirtschaft und Rüstung 1939–1945* (Düsseldorf, 1977). D. Ross, *Hitler und Dollfuss* (Hamburg, 1966); R. J. Smelser, *The Sudeten Problem 1932–1938* (Michigan, 1968); W. Schieder, *Der spanische Bürgerkrieg in der internationalen Politik* (Köln, 1974); A. Teichova, *An Economic Background to Munich* (Cambridge, 1976); Telford Taylor, *Munich* (New York, 1979), and J. T. Emmerson, *The Rhineland Crisis* (London, 1977), are some recent studies. In general, David Irving's *The War Path* (London, 1978) gives a good account of the crises as Hitler saw them.

Part 3

Original contributions to the history of the war, in recent years, have not been many — at least as regards Germany's part. David Irving's *Hitler's War* (London, 1977) is a useful up-to-date survey; John Erickson, *The Road to Stalingrad* (London, 1975), fills many gaps; John Lukács, *The Last European War* (London, 1977), is idiosyncratic and penetrating; Matthew Cooper, *The German Army: 1933–1945* (London, 1978); and, for the economic side, the works of Milward and Overy are irreplaceable. Comprehensive surveys of the war may be found in A. J. P. Taylor, *The Second World War* (London, 1974), and B. H. Liddell Hart, *History of the Second World War* (London, 1972). There is much of value, even for the historian of Hitler's Germany, in A. J. P. Taylor's *English History: 1914–1945* (reprinted, with updated bibliography, London, 1976). On other aspects of the war effort in Germany, there is Lucy Dawidowicz, *The War against the Jews* (London, 1975); Israel Trunk, *Judenrat* (New York, 1972); G. Reitlinger, *The Final Solution* (London, 1968); P. Hoffmann, *The German Resistance* (London, 1974). In German much can be gained from M. Broszat, *"Hitler und d. Genesis der Endlösung"* in *Vierteljahrshefte f. Zeitgeschichte*, 25 (1977); and especially Christian Streit, *Keine Kameraden* (Stuttgart, 1978), which shows the complicity of army authorities in atrocities — sometimes without Hitler's instructions or even knowledge. On the end of Hitler, H. R. Trevor-Roper, *The Last Days of Hitler* (New York, 1947), has not been replaced. A comprehensive bibliography for the war years, and the occupation generally, may be found in Norman Rich's *Hitler's War Aims* (cited above).

Index